PENN STATE NITTANY LIONS
Where Have You Gone?

KEN RAPPOPORT

www.SportsPublishingLLC.com

ISBN: 1-58261-893-3

Interior photos courtesy of the Penn State University Archives, Special Collections Library, unless otherwise noted

Publishers: Peter L. Bannon and Joseph J. Bannon Sr.
Senior managing editor: Susan M. Moyer
Acquisitions editor: Mike Pearson
Developmental editor: Doug Hoepker
Art director: K. Jeffrey Higgerson
Dust jacket design: Joseph Brumleve
Project manager: Greg Hickman
Imaging: Heidi Norsen and Dustin Hubbart
Photo editor: Erin Linden-Levy
Vice president of sales and marketing: Kevin King
Media and promotions managers: Mike Hagan (regional),
     Randy Fouts (national), Maurey Williamson (print)

Printed in the United States of America

Sports Publishing L.L.C.
804 North Neil Street
Champaign, IL 61820

Phone: 1-877-424-2665
Fax: 217-363-2073
www.SportsPublishingLLC.com

For Bernice,
My best gal and best pal

CONTENTS

FOREWORD

It's difficult to be nostalgic when you can't remember anything! Not remembering is a product of the aging process, for which I qualify. That's one reason why Ken Rappoport's latest Penn State Nittany Lion treatise, *Penn State: Where Have You Gone?*, is so thoroughly enjoyable. I'm familiar with all of the Nittany Lions that Ken has chronicled; watched and talked about 26 of them from the radio broadcast booth and interviewed most of those on the television series, *TV Quarterbacks*. And would you believe I broadcast the high school games of Dick Hoak and Roger Kochman in western Pennsylvania!

I am flattered that Ken asked me to write this foreword. I've been a fan of his for a long time. This book is just plain fun to read; makes you smile, makes you proud, makes you want to come back for more. For me it's a revisit of the most enjoyable days of my life: my tenure as the "Voice of Penn State Football." I believe I'm a better person for having had an association with a great football program, a great coach and a great university.

Over the years I have lost track of so many of these players. How gratifying it is to learn that each is making his mark off the gridiron. When I think of what Penn State football means to thousands and thousands of people, I realize how important it is to have a work like *Penn State: Where Have You Gone?* It's a must for all Penn Staters. More than that, it's a book that should interest all football fans. Sure, it's a Penn State story, but one that certainly enhances the image of college football in general. Thanks, Ken, for another superb book!

—Fran Fisher

ACKNOWLEDGMENTS

When I took on the assignment of writing this book, contacting dozens of former Penn State players seemed like a daunting task. It was, but fortunately the players made it easier for me. At the end, I managed to reach 41 and I want to thank all of them for so generously sharing their time and memories. I am especially indebted to Sam Stellatella and Chuck Franzetta, who opened doors for me and exemplified the true spirit of Penn State football. I also want to thank Mike Pearson at Sports Publishing for the assignment, Doug Hoepker for his editing, and my amazing wife Bernice for being my main support at home.

INTRODUCTION

They came. They saw. They hugged.

The occasion: the reunion of the 1959 Penn State Liberty Bowl team. Some 30-odd members had gathered at State College in the fall of 2004, 45 years after making history with their 7-0 triumph over Alabama—Penn State's first bowl victory. It was also the only time that Penn State beat a Bear Bryant-coached team.

In 1959, they were the young lions of Penn State, the toast of the town in State College. Now they are high school teachers, coaches, investment brokers, and retirees— just a bunch of old pals getting together to reminisce, tell tall tales and catch up on each other's lives.

"You could see the affection we have for each other," said Sam Stellatella, a Penn State lineman and kicker from 1957-59 who is the one-man committee for the reunions.

Not even a hurricane could keep them away. Ivan had wreaked havoc over a good part of the eastern United States. On the night before the game, the rain came down harder than a linebacker's blitz. Much of the surrounding area was flooded, and roads were blocked.

Still they came.

By Saturday morning, the skies had cleared, and sunshine warmed things up. The Reunion Boys met in the Lettermen's Lot early before heading over to the stadium. At halftime the Liberty Bowl players were introduced to the fans and received a warm ovation. Following Penn State's 37-13 victory over Central Florida, the players gathered in a banquet room at the Nittany Lion Inn.

Stellatella warmed up the crowd by playing a videotape from the 1959 season. For a while, the players were transported back in time. There was quarterback Richie Lucas, young and trim again, spinning and cutting for large gains. There was fullback Pat Botula, the team captain, blasting through for vital yardage.

And no highlight reel would be complete without some footage of the Nittany Lions winning the inaugural Liberty Bowl Game in Philadelphia. For the record, Roger Kochman scored on a pass from Galen Hall, substituting for the injured Lucas, for the only score of the game. Hall was the first to speak at the banquet. Now an assistant coach at Penn State, Hall talked about the current "young" Nittany Lion team. He figured the Lions were "about a year away" from greatness.

Next Botula talked about the Penn State experience. To him, it was more than just going to college—it saved his life. His Penn State dorm room was nicer than the house he lived in, he said. He didn't know how he would have survived without Penn State.

Today Botula is doing all right for himself. He is an investment counselor in Pittsburgh, handling hundreds of millions of dollars.

"You have to remember, a lot of these guys came from steel mill towns, and coal mining towns," Stellatella said. "A lot of these guys were dirt-poor. I don't think some of them had indoor plumbing, and of course, football was their ticket out of poverty, and they all did very well for themselves."

Stellatella was next. He talked about Frank Korbini, who had suffered a heart attack that morning. Stellatella had brought a team jacket for Korbini, and later presented it to him in the hospital.

By the end of the program, the players said their goodbyes with hugs and handshakes. For many of them, that would have to do until the next reunion in five years. That would be the 50th anniversary in 2009—the Big Five-0.

Indeed, Stellatella was already looking forward to that one.

"It's a labor of love for me," he said.

Enjoy the following stories of some of the players from that notable Liberty Bowl team, along with dozens of others from many different eras. Some of the players are well known, others less familiar but equally important. And all of them share the same glowing legacy. In a manner of speaking, it is a pride of lions.

Once upon a time they played football for Penn State.

JEFF DURKOTA

They came down the snowy slope firing rifles. It was warfare in the mountains of Italy during the Second World War and Jeff Durkota was right in the middle of it.

"We fought in the snow, on skis, in the Apennine Mountains," Durkota recalls. "We fought there all winter, and then in the spring we spearheaded the drive across the Po Valley and went up through Bologna, Moderno, Verona, and then Lake Garda."

Like many other young American men of the 1940s, Durkota's college football career was divided by the war. In 1941, Durkota was a promising running back from western Pennsylvania on Penn State's undefeated freshman team. The next year he was on the varsity under Bob Higgins as the Lions went 6-1-1. It wasn't too long, though, before Durkota would be firing rifles instead of firing footballs. He took a part of his training in the Rocky Mountains of Colorado. Then it was on to Italy.

"We went over in December of '44," Durkota recalls. "We spent Christmas in Naples. From there we went to Pisa, and then from there we started to fight in the Apennine Mountains.

"I was in the 10th Mountain Division—ski troops. You've heard of the 10th now. They're pretty well known, because they were in Afghanistan. You had to join. You had to write and be accepted. It took three letters of recommendation before they accepted you."

When he came back to Penn State in 1946, Durkota went out for football again, joining a veteran group.

"I would say 50 percent, maybe 60 percent of the players who played before the war were back," Durkota remembers. "They were all bigger. When I played in my junior year, I weighed 195 (up from 170 in his freshman year). And that's why we had such a good team. We were bigger, smarter."

In 1947, Penn State took an unbeaten team into the Cotton Bowl. Talk about that particular team and it's usually the defense that comes to mind, and for good reason. All-American Steve Suhey was a key defensive player for the Lions as Penn State established a strong defensive identity. The 1947 team still holds NCAA records for fewest yards allowed in a game (minus-47 against Syracuse), fewest average yards allowed for a season (17.0 per game) and fewest average yards allowed per rush (0.64) over the course of a season.

The offense wasn't bad, either.

"We didn't pass too much back then, but we were a powerhouse," he says. "We just plugged away, made our two yards, five yards, seven yards. We were big and strong. We just bolted our way through. It was an awesome team."

JEFF DURKOTA

Years lettered: 1942, 1946 and 1947
Position: Running back
Achievements: He led the Lions in touchdowns in 1947 with 10.

Durkota led the Nittany Lions in touchdowns that year, by his count "11 or 12, both rushing and passing." (The actual number in the record books is 10.)

The Lions were a machine, beating opponents by scores like 75-0 (over Fordham) and 54-0 (against Bucknell).

The great disappointment for Durkota and the Lions that season was a 13-13 tie with Southern Methodist University in the Cotton Bowl. The tie spoiled a perfect record for one of Penn State's greatest teams ever.

Coming into the Cotton Bowl game, Penn State had shut out six teams and outscored the opposition by a composite 319-27.

"Eddie Czekaj missed the extra point, so we always kid him about losing the game," Durkota says.

Offensively, one of Durkota's biggest afternoons came in the Lions' drubbing of Fordham.

"I think I had five or six touchdowns when we played Fordham," he says.

It was not, however, his most memorable afternoon.

"I think one of our better games was Navy," recalls Durkota of the 20-7 win. "We played down in Baltimore in the mud. It rained the whole game and we beat them. I made two touchdowns that game. I ran a lot of reverses."

After college, Durkota was drafted by two professional teams—the Philadelphia Eagles of the National Football League and the Cleveland Browns of the All-American Football Conference. The AAFC then featured such teams as the Browns, Los Angeles Dons, San Francisco 49ers, Chicago Rockets, Buffalo Bills, Baltimore Colts, New York Yankees and Brooklyn Dodgers. Some of those teams would eventually join the NFL.

"I signed with the Browns because they had a prestigious name and they were the champs in the league every year," Durkota says.

It was with the Browns that Durkota got his first lesson in negotiating a contract.

"They offered a thousand dollars first, and I said no," Durkota remembers. "Then they offered me two thousand, and I took it. But later on, I found out they had a third check for three thousand, and I should have said no again, and I could have gotten the three thousand. But after the first no, I accepted the second offer.

"That was the bonus, and with that money, I bought a ring for my college sweetheart. We got engaged, then in December '48 we got married."

Durkota's stay with the Browns was short.

"They sold me to Buffalo because Buffalo was after me," he says. "Then, I had preseason training there and played a couple of exhibition games. I was playing in Chicago one night, and they told me I was traded to the Los Angeles Dons. So they gave me a check, I went back to Buffalo, and took off for LA. I liked Los Angeles very much. I played with the Dons for two years."

Durkota's career might have been short, but for him it was also sweet.

"I really enjoyed playing pro ball," says Durkota, whose yearly salary of $7,000 was pretty good money for the time. "Of course, then we played the Single Wing and we played 60 minutes. Back then, you played 60 minutes or you didn't make the team."

Durkota played professionally for a couple of years before going into private business. He currently has an automobile dealership, Brubaker Chrysler-Jeep, in Lancaster, Pennsylvania.

"That was the original name of this dealership," Durkota says. "When we bought it, we just kept the name."

That was about 50 years ago, and Durkota's auto business is still moving along at a good clip. At the age of 80, the seemingly tireless Durkota is still on the go.

Once a great runner, always a great runner.

WALLY TRIPLETT

Wally Triplett, one for the books. As one of the first African Americans to play in the Cotton Bowl and the first African American to be drafted by the National Football League, Triplett earned a singular distinction in American sports.

With the Detroit Lions, he put on one of the greatest one-man exhibitions in NFL history. They haven't forgotten about it in the Motor City, just as old-time alums still recall the record-making 1947 team at Penn State. Triplett played a featured part on that team's offense and defense.

"We got mad if somebody made two, three yards," Triplett says. "In fact, that used to be our cry and our pride: 'Give 'em nothing!' That kind of spurred us on.

"We played against teams back then that were known to score and run up big yards. But we held them to almost nothing."

For the record: the gritty 1947 Nittany Lions established the NCAA mark for fewest yards allowed in one game—minus-47 against Syracuse. They can also boast of the fewest rushing yards allowed over the season (an average of 17.0 over nine games) and the lowest average per rush (0.64).

You could look it up in the record books.

The Nittany Lions held opponents to a total of 27 points, while scoring 319 themselves en route to a 9-0 season. With his tackling ability in the backfield, Triplett was an important part of the defense. With his running ability, Triplett was an integral part of the offense. Hard to believe, but they played both ways then—which is why they called the players "60-minute men."

In the 1947 Cotton Bowl game against Southern Methodist University, Triplett played in 58 of the game's 60 minutes.

"You had to be in shape," Triplett remembers. "You appreciated timeouts. I kidded a guy on the Detroit Lions once when he had a dislocated finger. He called timeout. I said, 'Are you crazy? We never called a timeout for a dislocated finger, man. Pop it back in, and keep going.'"

Triplett still stands No. 2 all-time in career punt return average at Penn State with a mark of 16.5 yards. In 1948, Triplett returned one punt 85 yards against West Virginia. You could look that up, too.

"I remember I had a couple good runbacks and good pass receptions against West Virginia," Triplett says. "I scored the winning touchdown against them with an off-tackle play."

How sweet it was for Triplett, especially considering that the Mountaineers did not treat black players too kindly.

WALLY TRIPLETT

Years lettered: 1946, 1947 and 1948
Position: Tailback, punt returner
Achievements: No. 2 in career punt return
average at Penn State (16.5 yards)

"They were a rough team," Triplett says.

It was a sign of the times. As obvious as black and white, America was a segregated nation.

Many schools, particularly in the South, refused to allow blacks on their teams. That's why Triplett still gets a chuckle out of a recruiting letter he once received from the segregated University of Miami. Triplett then was a high school star in Elkins Park, a suburb of Philadelphia.

"They didn't know I was black," Triplett says. "They just took the all-suburban and all-scholastic and all-state [players] and sent them letters."

Triplett sent a letter back, explaining who he was, and that under the circumstances there was no way he could honor Miami's offer of a scholarship.

He received another letter from the university. This time, the athletic director apologized for the recruiting mix-up. He told Triplett not to be bitter, that integration would eventually happen, although "not in our lifetime."

"I laughed at that," remembers Triplett, "because, as the athletic director had put it, it would never happen in our lifetime. And he's spinning over in his grave right now. Anyhow, that was the attitude back then."

Triplett had attitude, too—enough to get by when the going got rough.

"I guess I was cocky," Triplett says. "I was able to take care of myself."

He admittedly got off on the wrong foot with coach Bob Higgins, the man everyone called "The Hig."

"He and I didn't hit it off, because he thought I was a rich, intellectual kid from suburban Philadelphia. He was used to—and wanted—all those poor, rough boys from western Pennsylvania."

Actually, Triplett didn't go to Penn State on a football scholarship. His was a senatorial scholarship, which made him stand out all the more among the players from the coal mining areas that Higgins preferred.

"I went up there and booked myself into a hotel, which kind of upset Hig when he heard about it. He said he had never heard of an athlete coming up and getting a hotel room."

On his way to his first meeting with Higgins, Triplett noticed that a bus station had a sign out looking for a dishwasher.

"I took the sign in and ended up with the job. The Penn State athletic department was always worried about where they were going to find players work and where players could eat. Most of the guys worked in fraternity houses. They would get their meals and pin money.

"So I had a job, and I could get my meals. That didn't set well with The Hig because he didn't have any financial control over me, until later on, when I made the team."

Segregationist policies were in effect even at Penn State, generally known as a liberal school when it came to race. Before Triplett made the team, he was told by Higgins that he had to room in Lincoln Hall, "where the colored athletes live." One of his roommates was Barney Ewell, one of America's great track stars.

Before long, Triplett himself became a star in his own right. And he was a trailblazer, too, along with Dennie Hoggard, the only other black on the 1947 Penn State team.

With their undefeated record, the Nittany Lions were an obvious choice to play in one of the major bowl games. The Rose Bowl was already set with representatives from the Pac-8 and Big Ten conferences. The other bowls were situated below the Mason-Dixon Line, a problem for teams that featured African American players.

The Cotton Bowl had an opening against Southern Methodist, another undefeated team. The Penn State players wanted to go. But not without their two black teammates.

"We all go, or nobody goes," was Penn State's motto.

"When Southern Methodist heard that, Southern Methodist said they would break their color barrier, which had been a traditional thing, and they would play us," Triplett says.

It was a liberal decision at the time, considering the circumstances.

"Miami had refused to play us in the Orange Bowl because of their restriction [against blacks]."

Triplett and Hoggard would therefore be making history as the first African Americans to play in the Cotton Bowl.

Now the question came up: where would the Penn State players stay? Since no hotels were available for blacks in town, Penn State arranged for its players to stay at a Navy base outside of Dallas.

"So it was a history-making game, both socially and athletically," Triplett says. "And the other part of it was, it gave an opportunity of breaking down the barriers in the segregation of the fans."

Hoggard's mother, the wife of a state senator, came to the game as part of the Pennsylvania state delegation.

"They had her sitting on the 50-yard line with everybody else," Triplett recalls. "That was a big thing."

The fans saw a game that was worthy of two undefeated teams. Penn State trailed 13-0 before rallying with two touchdowns. Triplett scored the second TD on a short pass from Elwood Petchell.

"We got behind early," Triplett says. "But we came back, and I was able to score the tying touchdown to make it 13-13. We missed the extra point and that's the way it stood."

Final: Penn State 13, SMU 13.

"Southern Methodist had been a high-scoring team. We were used to low scoring, so that didn't faze us."

To say Penn State was competitive during Triplett's time there from 1946-48 would be an understatement. During those three seasons, the Nittany Lions had a 22-3-2 record. They lost the three games by a total of just 17 points.

Even their scrimmages were impressive. One year they went up to West Point and beat Army, a national power featuring running greats Doc Blanchard and Glen Davis. And during the regular season they whipped Navy, another powerhouse, to spoil President Harry Truman's afternoon.

"He refused to come into the locker room," Triplett says.

Triplett went on to the pros and spoiled the day for several more opponents. How he got to the NFL is an interesting story.

"There were two leagues at the time," Triplett recalls. "The established one was the National Football League, a very prejudiced, old, rough league. And here comes this upstart league called the All-American Conference, which sought out a lot of the black kids from schools and started to try to compete with the NFL.

"So the NFL held mostly to their policy of discrimination, and they did not seek to draft anybody until the year I came along. And they relented and drafted me."

At the same time, Triplett was drafted by the Brooklyn football Dodgers, who were in the All-American Conference.

"Branch Rickey [the general manager] was so cheap. After discussing terms with him, I said I'll go ahead with Detroit. They were offering me a few more dollars. It was about a $700 difference. And so I went with Detroit."

By signing with the Lions, Triplett became the first black to be drafted in the NFL.

"They had blacks who played before, but they were always selected by coaches."

The people who ran the NFL would soon find out what they had been missing. As a rookie, Triplett set a Lions record with an 80-yard touchdown run from scrimmage against Green Bay. Then, on October 29, 1950, he had another record afternoon against the Los Angeles Rams.

"I had a good day," Triplett modestly recalls.

The five-foot-10, 173-pound running back returned four kickoffs for a team-record 294 yards. Featured was a 97-yard return for a touchdown, one of three he scored that day.

"I thought this was the easiest thing going," Triplett says with a chuckle. "If you average it out, I think it's 70-some yards [a return]."

It was the only bright spot of the day for the Lions, who were beaten by the Rams, 65-24. Triplett didn't even realize that he was setting a record at the time.

In 2003, Triplett was honored by the Lions, who named him an "alumni honorary captain" for one of their games, part of a yearly effort to remember former players.

Triplett's pro career was cut short by the Korean War.

"After the war I came back to Detroit," he says. "I had gotten married. Then I looked for a job."

Triplett did some teaching for a while, and at the same time worked in the insurance business. Purely by accident, he was involved in another breakthrough for blacks.

"The racing industry was beginning to prosper in Michigan and they didn't have any black clerks," Triplett says. "They had people cleaning toilets and everything—the menial stuff—but as far as handling the money, they didn't have any blacks.

"I happened to know the commissioner who was a former reporter for the now defunct *Detroit Times*. And when he heard about it, he made sure that I went down and put in an application. So I became the first black racing clerk. I didn't mean to. … I just did it to open the doors for somebody else. But, doggone it, I stayed with it, and that was part of my resume for 35 years."

Triplett also raised a family.

"We were blessed with four kids," Triplett says. "I lost one two years ago to cancer. The other day, I did the cancer walk for the City of Hope. I'm involved in various things like that now."

Meanwhile, sports fans haven't forgotten his contributions on the gridiron. And Triplett hasn't forgotten those great teams and friendships he forged at Penn State.

"We grew to be a great team together, because we had a mixture of kids like myself who were just coming in from high school, and we had a mixture of the war veterans who were coming back from the war," Triplett says. "And so we developed a camaraderie that enabled us to break down barriers … social barriers that became famous.

"And that's what we actually became famous for, because we began to develop an attitude that we all played or no one played."

Where Have You Gone?

CHARLES "JIGGS" BEATTY

Talk about a life taking funny twists and turns. Charles "Jiggs" Bailey had played football against pros before he ever stepped onto a college field. He went to college before he graduated from high school. As a Penn State center and linebacker in the 1940s, he once belted out opposing football players. Now this broad-shouldered ex-Nittany Lion and ex-Marine belts out "Lida Rose" as part of a barbershop quartet.

And his nickname? Well, that's a story, too.

He was just a little bald-headed baby when his grandfather walked into his room.

"That looks just like Jiggs," Beatty's grandfather said, making reference to a popular comic strip of the day, "Maggie and Jiggs."

The nickname stuck.

"If you called me Charles in a room, I wouldn't even pay attention to you," Beatty says.

Beatty, raised in Wayne, Pennsylvania, outside Philadelphia, had always wanted to go to Penn State "without knowing a thing about it, except I didn't like Penn."

He had left high school to enlist in the Marines for the Second World War. He then spent three years in the Pacific. When he wasn't carrying a rifle, he was carrying a football. He first suited up for teams that played regimental football at Guadalcanal after it was secured by the Marines; then, he played in the China Bowl, which matched two regiments against each other. Beatty said the teams included "a lot of pros."

"It was the first time anybody had seen football in China," Beatty recalls. "They didn't know what was going on. We played up in northern China, right after the bomb was dropped."

The atomic bomb had signaled the end of the war, and all of a sudden veterans were pouring into colleges under the GI Bill. A Penn State official said that as many as 60,000 veterans had applied to the school in one year.

When Beatty got home, he took off for University Park with a couple of letters of recommendation—one from a Philadelphia newspaperman and the other from his high school coach. Bailey didn't know it at the time, but his high school coach had been a teammate of Penn State coach Bob Higgins back in the old days.

Beatty found Higgins on the golf course, introduced himself and gave him the letters of recommendation.

"He stopped the golf game for a couple of minutes and read these two letters and put them in his pocket," Beatty says. "I had never read them. I felt they weren't for me to read."

Higgins directed Beatty to the admissions office and also told him, "Go on home and you'll hear from us."

CHARLES "JIGGS" BEATTY

Years lettered: 1947, 1948, and 1949
Position: Center-linebacker

"So I went home," Beatty says.

In about a month, he received a letter telling him to come up to University Park for summer practice. After that, he spent his freshman year at California (PA) State Teachers College. It was Penn State's policy then to send the freshman players there for a year of seasoning.

"I had never heard of it," Beatty says.

But pretty soon Beatty would make sure the school would hear of him.

"I was the captain of that team. It was the first undefeated team they'd ever had."

The next year, 1947, all those good freshman players were now sophomores.

"We went up to Penn State, all of us, and integrated with the rest of the people which, sometimes, was not easy. We thought we were pretty good. And of course, the upper class-men looked down on us as freshmen, which is understandable, I guess. And most of us were World War II veterans, so it was very interesting … frustrating on occasion, but very interesting.

"And it turned out to be a pretty good team when we got there."

"Pretty good" would be an understatement.

The hard-rock 1947 Penn State team went 9-0 in the regular season and set stunning defensive records that still stand.

"I can remember one official in a game after the other team ran a play," recalls Beatty. "They were mostly losing yardage. The official got us together quickly at the line of scrim-mage, and said: 'You guys are going to hurt each other, the way you're fighting over tack-les. You don't need to do what you're doing.'"

Practices were unusually bloody for the Nittany Lions. Sometimes the toughest teams they faced that year were in their own scrimmages.

"We would scrimmage Tuesdays, Wednesdays and sometimes on Thursdays, and put the ball down on the 35-yard line," Beatty says, "and nobody would move it more than 10 yards.

"We just ran it like a game. It was just very hard … sometimes there was no love lost."

At six-foot-one and 212 pounds, Beatty was one of the biggest players on the team.

"There were only three guys on the team that outweighed me," Beatty says. "Think about that—Joe Paterno's fast running backs today weigh 240 pounds, and the rest of the team is out of sight when you're standing in front of them."

A Higgins team relied heavily on the running game, mostly Single Wing.

"I think we only passed about three times a game," Beatty says.

In the Cotton Bowl against SMU, however, the Nittany Lions went to the air to score both their touchdowns in a 13-13 tie. Penn State fought back from an early 13-0 deficit to preserve its unbeaten season.

If not for a heartbreaking late-season 7-0 defeat by Pittsburgh in 1948, the Nittany Lions could have boasted of another unbeaten year. It was about this time that Beatty was called up to the Registrar's office at Old Main.

"He found out three years later that I never graduated high school," Beatty says. "I never went a day in what would have been my senior year in high school. And the regis-trar called me in and started to laugh. He said, 'Well, we can't throw you out of school. Besides, Higgins would cut my throat.'

Charles "Jiggs" Beatty is retired in Wilmington,
Delaware, and sings in a barbershop quartet.
Photo courtesy of Charles Beatty

"And the day before graduation, I got a big, official-looking paper from my high school. It was signed by the school superintendent, who was my home room teacher. She put a little note on it, saying, 'I guess if you can graduate from college, you can graduate from high school.' She put me in the top ten percent of the class."

Before graduating, however, Beatty had to make it through the 1949 season. Higgins had retired and Penn State slumped to a 5-4 record under Joe Bedenk, the longtime line coach who held the head coaching job for only one season.

"A lot of guys weren't happy with the change," Beatty says. "The Hig should have stayed one more year, and he even admitted that."

After graduation, Beatty sold insurance to the Penn State students for two years. He loved Penn State so much that he didn't want to leave. But eventually, he joined his father's contracting business in Wilmington, Delaware. That was around 1954. Beatty ended up owning the company, retiring in 1993.

"I worked until I was 69," he says.

As a hobby, he had been singing in a barbershop quartet for quite a while.

"This is my 40th year that I've been doing this," Beatty says. "I have a voice coach. I started six months ago. I should have done it 16 years ago. It really makes things better."

Beatty's group has been well established in the Wilmington area for some time.

"If you sing in a quartet, you get a little bit of a name," he says. "People call you up to come sing at weddings, parties, all kinds of stuff."

It's a wonder that Beatty finds the time for a hobby. He and his wife, Winifred, have 11 children, 23 grandchildren and three great-grandchildren to enjoy. Yet, in his spare time, he also sets up reunions for the 1947 Penn State football team.

That's the best part, he says—getting together with former teammates and friends and swapping stories about the good, old days. As part of a fabled team, there will always be good stories to tell.

JOHN "SHAG" WOLOSKY

He lives in a mining town nowadays without a mine, so small that it has no high school and he has no street address. Just write to "John Wolosky, Isabella, Pennsylvania," and the player from the great 1947 Penn State football team will get your letter.

"I worked in the mines here in the off season between the time I went to high school and went to college," Wolosky says. "The mine's worked out, but the village is still here."

Wolosky is the subject of one of the most memorable Penn State recruiting stories. Like fine wine, it keeps getting better with age. "Shag" Wolosky would probably swear on a stack of Nittany Lions media guides that it's true, no matter how unlikely it seems. And so the legend grows, just like Pinocchio's nose, every time he stands up to talk at a reunion of the 1947 team.

"I always thought the highlight of the reunion was for Shag to get up and tell us how he got to Penn State," says Negley Norton, who played on that elite team with Wolosky.

As the story goes, Wolosky was a highly prized high school player from western Pennsylvania. He played at Brownsville High, about six miles from Isabella. He had visited the Ohio State campus and was impressed. The Buckeyes had laid out their red and grey carpet for Wolosky. His chaperone for the visit was none other than Jesse Owens, the world-famous track star.

Wolosky had made up his mind: he was going to Ohio State.

"I got a letter from this Casey Jones to meet him in Greensburg," Wolosky remembers. "We were going to go to Ohio State. It was me and two or three other guys.

"We were to meet in Greensburg and go to State, the letter said."

Wolosky and friends piled into Jones's car. Next stop: Columbus. At least that's what they thought.

"Well, when we got in there, it was State College instead of Ohio State."

Norton embellishes the story a bit, by quoting what Wolosky usually says at those team reunions: "We all felt that we were going to Ohio State. We couldn't figure out why we were driving into the sun."

Adds Wolosky:

"I think we knew what was happening. But that's how we always told the story: that we were going to Ohio State and we ended up at Penn State."

Casey Jones, it turned out, was a scout for Penn State coach Bob Higgins.

That was 1941. And it was Penn State's gain and Ohio State's loss. Wolosky would eventually be part of one of Penn State's greatest teams, playing center and linebacker on the '47 Lions. Only a tie with SMU in the Cotton Bowl spoiled a perfect season for

JOHN "SHAG" WOLOSKY

Years lettered: 1941, 1942, and 1947
Position: Linebacker

Higgins's historic team. Wolosky, it turned out, saved the Lions from a loss in that game with a great defensive play.

"I happened to block Doak Walker's extra point," Wolosky says. "They were winning, and I said, 'Aw, heck, I'm going to go across there and see what I can do.'"

Wolosky came rushing over from his outside linebacker position.

"I moved myself over the center. And I jumped center just as he snapped, and I was standing there when Walker went to kick the ball. He just kicked it on the side.

"And then (after Walker's extra-point try was stopped) we decided to play some ball. We said, 'Heck, while we're down here, let's get together and play.' And we had a pretty good discussion at halftime. We controlled the ballgame in the second half."

Penn State rallied from a 13-0 deficit for a 13-13 tie. The Nittany Lions wound up with a 9-0-1 record and ranked No. 4 in the national polls.

The game had some social significance, too. For the first time in history, a black played football in the Cotton Bowl. Penn State had two black players—Wally Triplett and Dennie Hoggard. Many hotels and restaurants had a whites-only policy at the time of the Cotton Bowl.

"When we were going to go to the game, we had no place to eat," Wolosky remembers. "They wouldn't take us because of our black players. And so we had to go find a place outside of the city, and we were late for the game."

It was Triplett, incidentally, who caught a touchdown pass to tie the Cotton Bowl clash at 13.

"And before the game was over, the last play or two, we were down on their 10- or 15-yard line," Wolosky recalls. "Elwood Petchell threw a pass to Hoggard, and it hit him in the chest and dropped to the ground, and the game was over.

"I told him at various get-togethers later, 'Dennis, maybe it was a good thing you dropped that.' He said, 'Why?' I said, 'We would have had a hell of a time getting out of Texas.'"

Wolosky came to University Park with a talented freshman class.

"The '41 [freshman] team went undefeated, and we had a terrific ballclub," Wolosky says.

Many of those players would soon be serving in the Second World War. Wolosky was one of them. He was drafted by the Army after the 1942 season and served in Europe.

By 1946, Higgins was starting to put together a powerful team. The result was the 1947 squad that won nine regular-season games by an average of more than 32 points. Guard Steve Suhey, who would marry Higgins's daughter, was an All-America guard who starred on both sides of the ball in the era of two-way football. The Penn State line also featured Wolosky at center, Joe Drazenovich at the other guard position, Norton and John Nolan at tackles, and Sam Tamburo and John Potsklan at ends. The backfield featured Petchell, Jeff Durkota, Larry Joe, Fran Rogel, Triplett and Charles Drazenovich, Joe's brother. Ed Czekaj, who would later become the Penn State athletic director, was the team's kicking specialist.

"We played Fordham in New York that year," Wolosky remembers. "It was 55-0 at halftime. This was a strange ballgame. We were winning by 30-0 or 35-0 in the first quarter, and on first down we were punting because Higgins didn't want to run it up."

John "Shag" Wolosky, a retired teacher, lives in Isabella, Pennsylvania, with his wife, Margaret.
Photo courtesy of John Wolosky

"They would try to score, and we'd intercept and go for a touchdown. At halftime, it was 55-0 and still they were doing the same thing. It was one situation where as soon as we got the ball, they went back to receive. The whole second half was that way."

Final: Penn State 75, Fordham 0.

"It was all second-, third-, fourth-stringers playing for us," Wolosky says.

Following graduation, Wolosky played for the New York Giants "for a short time."

"Then I went to West Virginia," Wolosky says. "There was a Penn Stater who came after me and asked me if I would play with his independent team. They were a pro team, and they were pretty good."

Wolosky said he got "a little money" and a job as a carpenter's helper at a mill.

"The carpenter was making a dollar more an hour. I picked the wrong job."

Leaving the pro football life, Wolosky went into coaching football and baseball in high school near his hometown. He loved developing young players. He also loved developing their minds, and worked as a teacher for nearly 40 years before retirement.

"When you're in these schools, you teach everything," says Wolosky. "I taught history, then U.S. history, health, phys. ed., and then a little biology."

Wolosky and his wife, Margaret, have three children and two grandchildren. Today he goes to as many Penn State football games as he can. And he looks forward to the annual reunions of the 1947 team, at which time he will tell his recruiting story for the ages.

No matter how many times his teammates have heard it, it never gets old.

NEGLEY NORTON

"I've got a pile of stuff that I was going to make a scrapbook out of, but I haven't gotten around to it," says Negley Norton. "I'm too busy playing golf."

One thing is certain: Norton is enjoying retired life in Florida. He lives with his wife, Bette, in Bonita Springs, in the southwest corner of the state and doesn't miss the cold northern winters at all.

"I'm out on the golf course in the morning," says the onetime Penn State football player who anchored the line of the legendary 1947 team. "What we do is play golf early and we're done by noontime. In the afternoon you don't do much. It keeps you away from the heat."

More than 50 years removed from his glorious Penn State football days, Norton still keeps in touch with former teammates from the '47 squad. He attends reunions as often as he can.

"When we had our 50th reunion, they took us out on the field at halftime," Norton says. "To stand there and look up at this mass of people, it was unbelievable."

Beaver Stadium looked much different in Norton's time, of course. Crowds of 15,000 to 20,000 were common then, as opposed to the crowds of 100,000 today.

The campus was different, too, as Norton recalls.

"We used to play softball out in the fields on campus where buildings are today."

The hallmark of the '47 team was a rock-hard defense. With the mix of returning war veterans and outstanding young talent, the unbeaten Lions went to Penn State's first bowl game since the 1922 season.

"The practices were brutal," Norton recalls. "They used to carry players off the field once in a while because the scrimmages would get so tough."

Norton played four seasons at Penn State and developed into an outstanding tackle.

"I was one of the youngest fellows," Norton says, "I was 20 years old. But we had fellows who were 24, 25, the same age as a lot of your pro players today. I played between Steve Suhey and John Nolan, and Steve was three or four years older than I was. You had the older fellows who kept the younger fellows going and the younger fellows kept making the older fellows play harder."

To Norton, the '47 Lions were the true definition of the word "team."

"There were no stars," Norton says. "We all hung out together. At the time, there was Graham's AC on Allen Street, right at the corner. And there used to be a bench out there. And in order to sit on the bench, you had to be a letterman. There was a lot of tradition to it. It was across from the Corner Room, and we all hung out there. None of us had any

NEGLEY NORTON

Years lettered: 1944, 1947, 1948 and 1949
Position: Tackle

Negley Norton, retired after a long career in sales,
is now a full-time golfer in Bonita Springs, Florida.
Photo courtesy of Negley Norton

money, because we didn't get much on the GI bill. And we just palled around together. They had a football house, and most of the guys lived there."

Norton had played varsity ball as a freshman at Penn State in 1944. It wasn't uncommon for the times, since the older players had been drafted for the war. In one game Norton recalled that Higgins was forced to start an all-freshman team.

After serving in the Army himself in 1945 and 1946, Norton returned to Penn State for spring practice in 1947. No matter how tough the practices, there was no swearing allowed. That was coach Bob Higgins's rule.

"If he caught you swearing in a practice, you were out," Norton says. "You just didn't do that, because he said if you did that in a game you'd be thrown out. And guys would get up off the pile and say something to one of the guys and Higgins would just be right on top of you."

There was a strict dress code then for the Penn State team, whether in the classroom or on the road.

"The line coach, Joe Bedenk, taught classes. When you came into his class, if you wore your letter sweater, you failed the course. You wore a shirt and a tie and a coat. And when we traveled, we had to go over to Lewistown to get the train. First we would go up to Rec Hall to get the bus, and Joe would stand outside. If you didn't have a shirt and tie on, you didn't get on the bus."

The Nittany Lions ran roughshod over most of their opponents in 1947. A few samples: 75-0 over Fordham, 54-0 over Bucknell and 46-0 over Colgate. They shut out six opponents and allowed a mere total of 27 points over nine games.

The Nittany Lions went on to the Cotton Bowl and played a fiercely fought 13-13 tie with a great SMU team. With a 9-0-1 record, Penn State claimed its first Lambert Trophy for supremacy in the East.

Norton never played on a better team at Penn State, although the '48 team came close with a 7-1-1 mark. In 1949, the Lions went 5-4 under Bedenk, who had replaced the retired Higgins. That was Norton's final season at Penn State.

"I was drafted by the different leagues at that time," Norton says. "I was drafted by the Philadelphia Eagles of the National Football League and then the Cleveland Browns of the All-American Conference. And the two leagues merged, and the next thing I knew the Pittsburgh Steelers had my name."

But Norton couldn't support a family on what they were paying pro football players in those days.

"There was no such thing as million-dollar contracts. Matter of fact, they didn't even pay you to sign. There was just no money there."

He went into the business world where he worked in sales until five years ago. Along the way, he witnessed pro football develop into a billion-dollar business.

After Norton retired, he and his wife moved to Florida. They have a son and two grandchildren living in Texas. The only time Norton might think of traveling back up north would be for a reunion of the '47 team, he says. The team had its 57th reunion in the summer of 2004.

Whenever Norton goes back to University Park, it's like old times: A bunch of buddies hanging around and telling tales, just like they used to do at Graham's AC on Allen Street.

JOE DRAZENOVICH

Joe Drazenovich had just returned from a fishing trip to Canada in the summer of 2004.

"I have a group of guys that call me and we've been going over the last 20 years," Drazenovich says. "It's a good group, and everyone does his share of work."

The fishing buddies usually go to the same spot—a secluded section of river in Ontario.

"The main base camp is probably 15 miles away," Drazenovich says. "So we're the only ones on the river for 15 miles south and 15 miles north. We have all the fish to ourselves. We keep some, we eat some, and we throw a lot back."

No TV. No radio. No problem.

"In the summer it gets dark later, and you fish a little later," Drazenovich says. "Sometimes you come in early and play Euchre (a card game similar to bridge)."

There's plenty of teamwork on the river.

"In case of a problem, there's somebody ready to help."

Not unlike the football teams that Drazenovich played on at Penn State in the '40s. One team in particular, the '47 Nittany Lions.

"We were pretty much geared to stopping opponents at the line of scrimmage, make them punt the ball, give us the ball, and then we'd systematically go and score," Drazenovich says.

The '47 Lions could make a case as the greatest defensive team in school history. Make that NCAA history. They still hold the NCAA record for fewest yards allowed in one game—minus 47 against Syracuse. Also, fewest yards allowed rushing over the season (an average of 17.0 over nine games) and lowest average per rush (0.64).

"We did a lot of blitzing, we did a lot of in and out, a lot of slants," recalls Drazenovich, an inside linebacker on defense and guard on offense. "As a result, we made tackles on the other side of the line instead of making tackles on our side."

The Lions outscored their opponents that season, 319-27. Drazenovich was an instrumental part of that team. He was among four regulars who came out of Brownsville High School in western Pennsylvania. The others: Drazenovich's brother, Chuck; John "Shag" Wolosky, and John Potsklan. Earl Bruce, the Brownsville coach, was helpful in getting them all to Penn State.

Drazenovich played some football at Penn State in 1944 before enlisting in the Air Force. It wasn't until 1945 that he was called up. He learned to be an airplane engine mechanic, serving 15 months in the United States and Europe. He returned in 1947,

JOE DRAZENOVICH

Years lettered: 1947, 1948 and 1949
Position: Linebacker and guard

along with many other veterans. Like other ex-servicemen who played football, Drazenovich went to college at the government's expense.

"You didn't get a lot in scholarship," Drazenovick says. "The GI Bill helped put us through. That's what helped the program get started there."

The returning players were more like men than boys, having survived a war. Plus, they had the experience and the technique learned from previous seasons.

"They thought maybe like a pro player would think today," Drazenovich says.

Drazenovich played at five-foot-10 and a "rock-hard 205." He also played lacrosse, but it was football that left a lasting impression. Especially playing for Bob Higgins.

"Higgins was not a loud individual," Drazenovich remembers. "He was very controlled … a good organizer, too."

Like a wartime general, Higgins laid out the battle plans for practice for these World War II veterans. Line coach Joe Bedenk was similar to a top sergeant.

"We had a great deal of respect for Bedenk," Drazenovich says. "Bedenk was a great line coach. He liked to see you do things with the right technique—get under and make contact and drive through your opponent. The linemen would go pretty hard at one another."

When a team scored as many as 14 points against Penn State, as West Virginia did, it was an anomaly.

"I think we took everything for granted, and maybe we got a little careless in that game," Drazenovich says. "But we survived, 21-14."

Then came an appearance in the Cotton Bowl against SMU. That was closer.

"I think they were about as tough a team as we played," Drazenovich says.

SMU featured Doak Walker, one of college football's all-time greats. And the Nittany Lions and Mustangs put on an all-time great battle. Trailing 13-7 at the half, the Nittany Lions realized they had their work cut out. Drazenovich recalled the conversation in the locker room:

"I don't remember the exact words, but I think Steve Suhey commented that we didn't come down here to lose. We're a better team than what we're showing. Let's get our act together and see that this job is done right. And we came out with a lot of enthusiasm and renewed effort, too.

"None of us at halftime felt we were going to lose."

Late in the third period, Petchel connected on a touchdown play with Wally Triplett to tie the score at 13. Ed Czekaj missed the extra point that would have given Penn State the lead. At least that's how the referee saw it. Drazenovich saw it differently.

"I will say this: 'til my dying day, I thought the extra point was good."

He was in good position to see the kick, blocking from his guard position and looking straight at the goalposts.

"At the time, the goalposts weren't as high as they are now," Drazenovich says. "They were only three, four feet above the crossbar."

Drazenovich remembered seeing Czekaj's kick go through the uprights and veer to the right. He believed the referee just assumed that the kick was wide right all the way.

"To this day, I say if we had jumped up and down like it was good, I'll bet we would have convinced the official back there that it was good. And, of course, we dropped a pass in the end zone, too."

Joe Drazenovich, a retired teacher, lives in Wexford, Pennsylvania, with his wife, Dorothy, and enjoys going on fishing trips to Canada.
Photo courtesy of Joe Drazenovich

That would be the pass from Petchel to Dennie Hoggard in the final seconds. Hoggard was well covered, and his vision of Petchell's pass was obscured. The ball hit his hands and his stomach and dropped to the ground.

The teams wound up in a 13-13 tie, spoiling Penn State's perfect season.

After school, Drazenovich went into the teaching profession in Pennsylvania and married his college sweetheart.

"Probably the most important thing that happened to me at Penn State was a lady that I met there, that I've been with since 1947," Drazenovich says, speaking of his wife, Dorothy.

They live in Wexford, Pennsylvania, "about 500 yards from where Dorothy was raised."

Their son, Andy, and daughter, Carol, both attended Penn State. Andy was a center on the 1978 Penn State team that played in the Sugar Bowl.

Drazenovich watches Penn State football whenever he can. He thinks the well-coached '47 team would match up well with today's teams—if nothing else than in knowing how to play the game. And certainly in heart and determination.

"We were strong, we were quick and fast, and we loved the game," Drazenovich says.

MILT PLUM

H is statistics are impressive, considering the run-oriented style of pro football played then: 17,536 passing yards and 122 touchdowns in 13 NFL seasons. At one time, Milt Plum held the record for passing percentage in the NFL.

"I'm third now," Plum says. "I was first for about 17 years. Then Joe Montana broke it and then Steve Young broke his, so I dropped to third last time I heard."

At Penn State in the mid-'50s, he was a fine, do-everything player. Plum played on both sides of the ball, as a quarterback on offense and safety on defense. He also kicked off, booted field goals and punted.

He was the Energizer Bunny long before there was such a thing.

"I didn't leave the field too often," Plum says by phone from his home in North Carolina. "Somebody told me I had the most time played in nine games one season."

In the pros from 1957-69, he was an All-Pro quarterback while playing mostly with the Cleveland Browns and Detroit Lions.

"The Browns, of course, had Jim Brown," Plum says. "They wanted somebody, a ball-handler, so to speak. Not that I was exceptional, but I could handle the ball well. And we weren't going to throw the ball. When it came down to a third down, we threw the ball."

Funny thing, all this would have never happened if Plum had followed his childhood dream of being a baseball player. A standout athlete at Woodbury High School in South Jersey, Plum was recruited for football by several schools, including Penn State.

"I didn't know what to do," Plum says. "My heart was in baseball. So I fiddled around and fiddled around.

"I think it was like late June before I called up the football office at Penn State and said I'd accept their scholarship. I think they were surprised. I think they kind of gave up on me. If I hadn't gotten a scholarship, I probably wouldn't have gone to college."

Plum fully intended to play baseball at Penn State as well as football. But the competition for quarterback was so fierce that spring football practice took priority. Baseball eventually went by the boards.

"There were always three quarterbacks fighting it out," he says.

Plum would eventually gain control of the Penn State team and play in some momentous games for the Nittany Lions—like 1956 at Ohio State.

"We went down there on Friday and Ohio State coach Woody Hayes had a show. And he spoke about Penn State for about three minutes, and then got on to the following week's game with Texas Christian. ... like, Penn State is coming to town, but next week, we've got TEXAS CHRISTIAN!.

MILT PLUM

Years lettered: 1955 and 1956
Position: Quarterback, safety and punter
Accomplishments: In 1956, he led the Lions in
passing (675 yards, 6 TDs) and interceptions (7).
In 1955, he tied for the interception lead (2).

"So I think it got a few guys mad. And then the next morning we had our pregame meal and I was one of the last out of the restaurant to board the bus. And the hostess said, 'Well, boys, give it the best you can.'"

The Nittany Lions did better than that. They beat the Buckeyes, 7-6.

"We weren't supposed to win. An eastern team just doesn't beat a Big Ten team. That was written in stone," Plum says. "I wanted to go back to that restaurant after the game so bad and say to the woman, 'Was it good enough for you?'"

Plum, who had a 72-yard punt against Ohio State, remembered that the Nittany Lions were much the worse for wear after that game.

"We took the train back and I'll tell you, we were banged up. It looked like one of those old Civil War movies … everybody lying around with legs propped up and bandages."

Then there was the 21-20 victory over Syracuse in 1955. Penn State coach Rip Engle said Plum gained "great stature" in that game.

"The only thing with that, I caught Jim Brown," Plum recalls. "He was off to the races. I had an angle on him and I was able to get him."

Plum remembered another Syracuse game, for another reason. It was his senior year and the Nittany Lions were locked in another typically epic struggle with their longtime rivals.

"They had a rule that if you started the game and came out, you could go back in that quarter," Plum says. "If you didn't start that quarter, say you went in and came out, you didn't go back in that quarter.

"Near the end of the game, we were down 13-9 and Rip Engle pulled me out to give me instructions for when we got the ball back. We got the ball back. I went back on the field, and [Syracuse coach Ben] Schwartzwalder said, 'Twenty-two is illegally substituted.' My number was twenty-two."

Officials took Plum by the arm and walked him off the field, no questions asked.

"Rip went beserk. First he turned to me and said, 'Are you illegally substituted?' I said, 'No! I've been in the whole game! First half, second half, until just three plays ago.' But I was out, and we lost 13-9."

With Plum a force on defense as well as offense, the Lions were usually on the winning side. Plum remembered when he picked off seven passes in one season from his "rover" safety position. And he could have had more.

"I knocked down two on purpose because they were fourth-down passes."

Plum would later become teammates with Brown, considered by some to be the greatest runner in NFL history. The Browns then were a run-oriented team, in many ways like the Penn State teams Plum played on.

"We didn't throw the ball in those days, not like nowadays," recalls Plum, a good size for a quarterback in his day at six-foot-two and 185 pounds. "I mean, these guys today throw the ball more in the first quarter than I did in four quarters."

In 1956, Plum's best year statistically at Penn State, he led the team in passing with 675 yards. He only threw 75 passes all season, six for touchdowns as the Lions went 6-2-1.

"Bill Kane probably had the best hands," Plum recalls of the player who led Penn State in pass receiving in 1955 and then both rushing and receiving in 1956.

When Plum went to camp with the Browns, he was pretty low on the depth chart. He wasn't sure where he stood—even after he made the team.

"In my rookie year there were seven of us in camp," he remembers. "They dropped one or two and they picked up a couple more. I threw every third day, because the No. 1 guy got 80 percent of the work.

"They never did tell me I made the team. We came back from the West Coast and coach Paul Brown never said boo to me."

After getting into nine games in the 1957 season, Plum played all 12 games in 1958. It was the start of a long-running pro career for him that featured dozens of sparkling Sundays. He made the Pro Bowl two years running, in 1960 and 1961. In 1960, he had his best season in passing percentage, with 60.4, and was intercepted only five times in 12 games. In 1961, he racked up his highest yardage total at 2,416.

After spending five years with the Browns, Plum played six more in Detroit. He was then traded to the Los Angeles Rams and almost didn't go. It was 1968 and he was thinking about retiring.

"My kids were getting to the point in school," Plum says, "and I was moving them from one school to another . . . half a year here, half a year there."

Then he got a call from Allie Sherman of the New York Giants and gave it one last try.

"It was very bad," Plum remembers. "They fired Sherman in the last exhibition game and they put Alex Webster in control that year. And we lost like the first seven games. It was just a bad year. It was time to get out."

Plum finished with a career completion percentage of 54.0.

Upon retirement from the NFL, he held a variety of jobs, including a sales position in the wood products industry. He said he chose to settle in North Carolina, "because that's where all the wood is."

He eventually quit the nine-to-five working world and began spending more time enjoying his golf and tennis games, and with his family. Plum has three children and five grandchildren. One of his grandchildren plays volleyball, basketball and softball in high school. Others are into baseball and soccer.

Just like their quick-footed grandfather, they're tough to pin down.

Milt Plum, retired in North Carolina after a successful pro football career, poses with Joe Paterno.
Photo courtesy of Milt Plum

Where Have You Gone?

JACK
SHERRY

Here's an interesting Penn State trivia question: Who is the only athlete in school history to letter in football and also captain a Final Four basketball team?

Jack Sherry is the answer.

"I'm sure that's never happened before or since," says Sherry, who played both sports at Penn State in the 1950s.

Sherry, actually, was a basketball player before he ever dreamed about playing football. How he got to suit up with the Nittany Lions football team is one of those serendipitous stories.

"I was very lucky," he says. "I wasn't a particularly tough kid."

It was the early 1950s and Sherry was a top-flight basketball player with West Catholic High School in Philadelphia, a hotbed of high school roundball then.

"Philadelphia basketball was probably the best in the world in those days," he says. "You had Tom Gola, Paul Arizin, Ernie Beck, Wilt Chamberlain, Guy Rodgers . . . I could go on and on. I played against better guys in the playground than Penn State had."

Sherry did play one year of high school football and then some sandlot football under Dave Defillipo, who earned a reputation coaching the legendary Pottstown Firebirds.

"I was basically a defensive back for him, and then he put me in at end and I caught a couple of touchdown passes," Sherry recalls.

To his surprise, Sherry got a football scholarship to Penn State because his high school coach, Mike Kerns, had ties there with Sever Toretti and Jim O'Hora, Penn State line coaches. All three had played football for the Nittany Lions.

"Back in those days, there was no television, so it was all word of mouth," Sherry says. "So Kerns recommended me, and I had only played one year of high school football.

"And all I could do was catch the ball. I had good hands. Most basketball players had good hands, so I caught a lot of touchdown passes. But I wasn't tough defensively in blocking and tackling, that sort of thing.

"So I went up to Penn State. Toretti met me at the bus and I think he wanted to throw up. He got this big skinny guy with pegged pants, the jacket collar up. I looked like a bad edition of the Fonz. Skinny as hell, a good athlete, but not a tough kid."

If not for the football scholarship, Sherry could not have afforded to go to Penn State.

"I'm the oldest of six kids," Sherry says. "My dad was a motorman. We grew up in Depression and World War II days, so none of us had any money. None of us. The rich kids didn't have money!"

JACK SHERRY

Years lettered: 1952, 1953 and 1954
Position: Safety, end
Accomplishments: Tied for the team lead in
receptions (11 for 160 yards) in 1954. Intercepted
eight passes in 1952 to set a new school record.

It was winter when Sherry first arrived on the Penn State campus, and basketball, not football, was the sport of the moment. He was asked to join his dorm team. It wasn't long before he was invited to play for the Penn State freshman basketball team.

"I started that week," Sherry recalls, "and I was the high scorer the rest of the year. That's how bad Penn State basketball was."

Then Sherry went out for spring football and things were a little different.

"They didn't even invite me back the following fall. That's how bad I was. I was overwhelmed with the toughness. They had me playing end, and I didn't have any freshman background, so I was thrown to the wolves. I remember walking out on the field and Toretti chewing me out because I walked out on the field. I didn't know any difference.

"We dressed in that water tower, which is right next to Rec Hall. I looked like something out of a bad George Gipp movie, big khaki pants that were drooping and sweat socks that drooped, and so forth."

But he was smart enough—a good student.

"I got a scholarship, so they had to put up with me," he says. "I went back there that fall and just got the heck beat out of me the whole fall. I was on the Foreign Squad, they call it today. Then it was the Suicide Squad. You were a different position every week, whoever you played. I was the Rutgers end, I was the West Virginia end, and so forth."

Sherry said he had "a terrible year in football." But he did go out for basketball, made the varsity and started.

"I was still only a second-semester freshman because you don't go into your third semester until about February. And our team went 17-1 at the start. It was unreal. And we went on the road and we lost three games by a total of eight points. Then we came back and won the rest of our games, and we went to the NCAAs in 1952."

The Nittany Lions were unfortunate to be paired in the first round against one of the great Kentucky teams of all time. Penn State lost despite 24 points from Jesse Arnelle, who also played football, and 10 from Sherry.

The game had side benefits for Sherry, though.

"One of the football coaches, Al Michaels, saw me playing basketball," remembers Sherry. "He said, 'The kid's fairly quick, he's fairly aggressive, I'm going to make him a safety.' Keep in mind I only played one year of high school football and one year of sandlot football, and now I was a safety."

Guess what? Sherry intercepted eight passes in the 1952 football season and shared a new Penn State record with backfield teammate Don Eyer. The interception record wasn't broken until 1969 when Neal Smith picked off 10.

"Most of the interceptions came because I was a good basketball player, I could follow the ball," Sherry says. "They didn't pass that well in those days. I played middle field. We had a three deep and Eyer was one of the guys on the side and Beetle Bailey was another one.

"I must have gone through two or three halfbacks who came and went. And I played every minute of every game on defense the rest of the year."

One of the season's highlights for Sherry: a 17-0 victory over Pitt in the final game of the season.

"That's the one I intercepted two passes and they gave me the interception record," Sherry recalls. "It was probably the highlight of my football career."

In his last two years, Sherry played end. In 1954, in a mostly ground-oriented offense, Sherry and Jim Garrity tied for the reception lead that year, each with 11 catches. Sherry averaged a spectacular 14.5 yards per catch that season.

"My last two years I had to play both ways, so I was an end both on offense and defense," Sherry says. "I always said there was never a time that I lined up that I didn't have a big, fat, ugly tackle or a big mean linebacker sitting over me, and I became a tough kid my senior year. I could block and tackle with the best of them. I played in the Blue-Grey Game and more than held my own."

He could also say the same for the NCAA basketball tournament. In the spring of 1954, Sherry captained one of Penn State's finest basketball teams. In the NCAA playoffs, the Nittany Lions advanced to the Final Four with victories over Toledo, Louisiana State and Notre Dame. Against Notre Dame, Sherry scored a personal-best 14 points. Penn State lost to a great LaSalle team featuring Tom Gola in the national semifinals before beating Southern Cal in the third-place game.

Following college, Sherry hoped to play either professional basketball or professional football, but "I wasn't good enough for the pros for either sport. Like the old cliché, you can't teach quickness and you can't teach height. And I didn't have either. I was a pretty good athlete, but that was it."

Sherry worked for Proctor and Gamble for a while before getting drafted into the armed services.

"I was all-Navy in basketball two times, captain of the Navy Olympic team and I captained the Navy AAU team. We won the All-Navy tournament, of which I am very proud."

Sherry started a career in sales with the American Seating Company, which produced seats for many of the sports stadiums and arenas in the country. After years of living in the Midwest, Sherry and his wife, Helen, returned to Pennsylvania. Now retired, Sherry has five children and 13 grandchildren.

Many years later, Sherry is still pinching himself about a series of fortunate events that made him a unique athlete at Penn State.

"I was basically a basketball player playing football," he says.

And a pretty good one at that, no matter the sport.

Jack Sherry is retired in Pennsylvania after a long career in sales.
Photo courtesy of Jack Sherry

DICK
HOAK

Just think of him as the Cal Ripken of football. Like the durable baseball star who broke Lou Gehrig's record of consecutive games played, Dick Hoak is on quite a streak himself. A onetime Penn State backfield star, Hoak took a job as an assistant coach with the Pittsburgh Steelers in 1972. He hasn't left yet.

"People ask me when I'm going to retire, and I say, 'I don't know,'" Hoak says. "I tell them, I still feel good, I still enjoy what I'm doing. It will be a year-by-year thing. I just coach, and when the year's over, I take a look at it. But right now, I have no plans of retiring."

The 2004 NFL season was Hoak's 33rd with the Steelers. Counting 10 years as a player, that made 43 years with one team! When the Steelers played their landmark 1,000th game as a franchise during the 2003 season, Hoak had been involved in 685 of them as a player and coach.

It's the same type of lion-hearted loyalty that he felt as a Penn State man.

"To me, it was four of the greatest years of my life," says Hoak, who has three children (all Penn State grads) with his wife, Lynn. "Playing for Joe Paterno and Rip Engle, they taught you other things beside football. They tried to teach you the right thing to do and how to behave. I really respected those people for that."

Now more than 700 games later as a player and coach for the Steelers, the games from his Penn State years seem to run together. But he won't forget one particular day against Oregon in the 1960 Liberty Bowl.

"I remember a lot about it," Hoak says. "I got the Most Valuable Player of the game award. I intercepted two passes, I scored two touchdowns and I threw for a touchdown. At that time you had to play both ways."

It was Hoak's going-away present to Penn State, resulting in an overwhelming 41-12 victory. Talk about an economical performance. Hoak, a quarterback on offense and safety on defense, didn't even start the game. Galen Hall did.

"At that time we had two units," Hoak says. "The first unit would play seven and a half, eight minutes of a quarter, and then the second string would go in and play seven and a half, eight minutes of a quarter. You couldn't have free substitution at the time."

Hoak came to Penn State out of Jeannette (PA) High School as a highly recruited quarterback prospect.

"Nobody in my family ever went to school, and the only way I was going to go was to get an athletic scholarship," Hoak says. "And when I was growing up, I always wanted to go to one of three schools, if I had the chance—Penn State, Ohio State or Michigan State."

Hoak did take the opportunity to visit other schools. But he finally decided on Penn State. It wasn't only because he liked the campus and that it was an easy drive from home.

DICK HOAK

Years lettered: 1958, 1959 and 1960
Position: Quarterback, halfback and defensive back
Accomplishments: Led the Lions in total offense in
1960 with 680 yards and six touchdowns.

"Most schools I went to, they take you to dinner, and then they give you to the football players to show you around," Hoak says. "Well, I followed college football. Most of the places I went, the guy who showed me around I had never even heard of.

"When I went to Penn State, Milt Plum showed me around. I knew who Milt was. He was a great quarterback, and I thought, well, these guys thought enough of me to give me to this guy. That had something to do with it, and they never pressured me, so that was the thing."

Hoak thought he was going to Penn State to be strictly a quarterback. Things suddenly changed.

"My sophomore year they were going to red-shirt me because they had the three quarterbacks back from the year before. And then a couple of the halfbacks got hurt leading up to the first game and here we go out to Nebraska and I'm returning the opening kickoff.

"I'm playing halfback as a sophomore. And then in my junior year, I also played halfback. Then my senior year I moved back to quarterback."

As a junior, Hoak played on the 1959 team that won Penn State's first bowl game. That year the Lions went 8-2 in the regular season and defeated Alabama, 7-0, in the first Liberty Bowl game.

"The '59 team was pretty good," Hoak recalls. "We lost by four points to Syracuse, which was the eventual national champion. Then Pitt upset us the last game."

Then in 1960, Penn State went 6-3 before meeting Oregon in the second Liberty Bowl game. Hoak led the Lions back from a 6-0 deficit, directing Penn State to three touchdowns in the second period. One of those he scored himself on a six-yard run that was described by a United Press International writer as a "ballet leap into the end zone." Coach Rip Engle called the touchdown play "one of the best individual performances I've seen."

Then in the fourth period, Hoak scored on an 11-yard run, tossed a 33-yard touchdown pass to Dick Pae and made two interceptions to help the Lions pull away from a 21-12 lead.

"Yeah, it was a nice day, it was a good day," Hoak recalls.

But a cold one. The game was played in sub-freezing temperatures on December 17, 1960 in Philadelphia.

"There weren't very many people at the game," Hoak remembers. "It was cold and there was snow in the stands. It was at the old Municipal Stadium, which seated 100,000. Only 17,000 showed up."

Hoak was hot, though. Gerry Farkas, a tackle who played on the so-called "Reddy Unit" most of the season with Hoak, called him "a very heady player… a gifted player in terms of being able to do a lot of things."

"He played running back for a good portion of his career at Penn State. Then they needed a quarterback for the Reddy Unit, and they switched him to quarterback," Farkas says. "It was amazing how well he could perform as a quarterback, and play defense, also."

Then it was goodbye to Penn State for Hoak, and hello to the Steelers, who selected him in the seventh round in the 1961 draft. Hoak's first pro game, an exhibition with the Baltimore Colts, left him shaking his head.

"I was from Penn State and we weren't allowed to swear," Hoak says. "In that first game with the Steelers, they called a penalty on us and you should have heard the swearing at the referee by our players and coaches. I thought, 'What did I get myself into?'"

*Dick Hoak has worked as an assistant coach
with the Pittsburgh Steelers since 1972.*
Photo courtesy of the Pittsburgh Steelers

That wasn't the only thing that surprised him about his first pro game.

"Late in the game we had a third down and I was thinking, 'I have to get this first down.' Bobby Lane was our quarterback and he was still in the game at the time. We were at the line of scrimmage and one of the Colts' linemen shouted out, 'Hey, Bobby, let's nobody get hurt and let's get out of here.' That's why I remember my first game."

For the next 10 years, Hoak starred in the Steelers' backfield, leading the team in rushing three times. The Steelers still struggled, however. Hoak remembered when the fans used to throw snowballs at the players as they ran out onto the field.

"They had two tunnels at Pitt Stadium, and we used to keep them guessing which tunnel we'd come out from each week," Hoak remembers.

After calling it a career, Hoak coached at a small high school in Wheeling, West Virginia, for a year. Then he came back to his home area to sign on as backfield coach for the Steelers.

Hoak's association with the Steelers is unprecedented among NFL coaches, usually a transient lot. In his time with the team, Hoak has coached some of the NFL's greatest players, including former Penn State running back Franco Harris and Jerome Bettis. For most of Hoak's career, the Steelers have ranked in the top ten in rushing in the NFL. In the 1970s, the Steelers won four Super Bowls and established themselves as one of the NFL's greatest dynasties.

Which is something that might also be said about Hoak, a one-man dynasty all by himself.

SAM STELLATELLA

"Let me show you some stuff," Sam Stellatella was saying in the livingroom of his home in Toms River, New Jersey.

He pulls out a Penn State football program from the 1950s, then a life-size cardboard cutout of Joe Paterno. Stellatella poses with his arm around the cutout.

"Want to take my picture?" he asks.

Stellatella is beaming. The Paterno cutout almost looks real.

Click.

Stellatella brings out more memorabilia, this from the '50s when he was considered the best high school player in New Jersey.

"This is my junior year. This is a cover for the magazine section for the *Newark News* ... this is the year I was selected the outstanding football player in the state."

Stellatella played for Nutley High School, a New Jersey powerhouse. He decided to attend Penn State "because they had a respectable football program and it was reasonably close to home." Good choice. With Stellatella as a linebacker, center and kicker, the Lions made history at the 1959 Liberty Bowl. That year they beat Alabama 7-0 for their first bowl victory and their only victory over a Bear Bryant-coached team.

"The Liberty Bowl was trying to get established," Stellatella says of the postseason game in Philadelphia. "They wanted to establish a major bowl game in the northeast. So they wanted Penn State to be in this game.

"We had a meeting . . . and we had a debate. Some of the guys wanted to hold out 'til after the Pitt game for one of the major bowls. We put it to a vote. We accepted the Liberty Bowl. Now psychologically, I don't know if that had an impact on us going into the Pitt game, but we had a terrible game and we were upset by Pitt (22-7)."

The Nittany Lions finished on a high note, though, by beating Alabama in the Liberty Bowl. Penn State's victory over the Crimson Tide was the first of four straight bowl appearances under Rip Engle. In 72 previous years of football, there had been a total of only two bowls for the Lions.

Penn State's fortunes started to swing with the undefeated freshman team in 1956, Stellatella's first year at Penn State.

"That freshman team was exceptional," Stellatella says. "And I always like to think that the freshman team in '56 established the foundation for the great football program that followed."

In Paterno, Stellatella saw the future of Penn State football.

"Joe was the quarterback coach and you could see back then as a young coach, he was brilliant. He was destined for great things."

SAM STELLATELLA

Years lettered: 1957, 1958 and 1959
Position: Linebacker, center and kicker

Sam Stellatella, retired teacher and coach, lives in New Jersey and serves as reunion chairman of the 1959 Liberty Bowl team.
Photo by Ken Rappaport

So were the Nittany Lions in the 1959 season, despite some bumps in the road. When they faced Syracuse on November 7, both were unbeaten and ranked in the Top Ten. The Orangemen were No. 4, the Nittany Lions, No. 7.

A crowd of 34,000 crammed into Beaver Stadium for Penn State's biggest game of the year.

"We received and went down and we scored," Stellatella remembers. "I missed the extra point . . . it was 6-0. Syracuse came back and they scored and kicked the extra point . . . 7-6. They had a powerful offense. And they were moving the ball pretty easily. And they scored again and it was 14-6.

"Then, in the second half they scored again, and they missed the extra point. So now it was 20-6. And they kicked off. We had a sophomore who was a sprint champion in Pennsylvania by the name of Roger Kochman. He took the ball one yard in the end zone, got a key block by Bud Colhouse, and went 101 yards to score. It was late in the game. We had to go for the two points. We didn't score. So it was 20-12."

Now there were just a couple of minutes left in the game.

"Syracuse was punting on their own 20-yard line. Andy Stynchula, who was a great lineman for Penn State and had a great pro career, came rushing through, leapt into the air, got hit, put his arm up and blocked the punt. We recovered on the one-yard line. We scored. It was now 20-18. We had to go for two points. We went for the two points and we don't score. We ended up losing 20-18 and Syracuse went on to win the national championship."

The Liberty Bowl game that season also had its share of drama.

"At the end of the season, Rip Engle always liked to put in a trick play to keep the guys interested," Stellatella remembers. "So we put in a fake field goal."

That, as it turned out, was a key play in the game against Alabama.

"It was freezing, it was windy," Stellatella says. "So we moved the ball well but couldn't score. And we went down and attempted a field goal and it was blocked. So now it was getting close to halftime and Alabama punted. They were deep in [their own territory], they were about on their own 20-yard line. And they were kicking in a gale wind. And the wind just took that ball and pushed it back . . . so we recovered the ball, with a couple of minutes to go, and we were on like the 20-yard line.

"So it was third or fourth down, almost the end of the half. The ball got snapped to Galen Hall, who was the backup quarterback for Richie Lucas. Lucas got hurt and was out. I came up and I faked the field goal. Galen Hall took the ball and he rolled out to the right.

"Kochman, who ran that 101-yard kickoff return against Syracuse, flaired out to the left. Hall threw the ball cross-country. Roger got the ball on about the five yard-line. He scored, and I kicked the extra point. So that was the only scoring for the game."

That was the final game for a fine group of Penn State players, many of whom wound up in the pros. While Penn State missed out on the national championship that season, Stellatella did eventually play on a championship team—in the military. Stellatella was a second lieutenant in the Army stationed at Ford Benning. One year, the Fort Benning team was the undefeated military champion.

After the service, Stellatella came back to New Jersey and had a long high school coaching career. One of his proudest achievements was his work as a defensive and conditioning coach with the St. Joe's freshman in Toms River.

"We were undefeated, untied, unscored-upon in six games against a tough schedule," Stellatella says. "To be unscored upon is a pretty good accomplishment at any level."

Stellatella also taught history and industrial arts in high school for 32 years, sold insurance and worked in the investing field. He keeps in touch with his former teammates as the reunion chairman of the Liberty Bowl team.

"We have a very, very close, tight team," he says.

Not surprising, considering the shared memories of all those thrilling seasons together and one breakthrough Liberty Bowl game in particular.

Where Have You Gone?

ROGER KOCHMAN

R oger Kochman tries to convince his high school sprinters that once upon a time he was as lean and quick as they are.

"I tell these guys, 'Hey, 45 years ago and 45 pounds ago, I was a sprinter, baby,'" Kochman says with a chuckle.

Actually, a little more than a sprinter. From 1959-62, Kochman was a top running back at Penn State and played a featured role in some of the Nittany Lions' most important football games of the era.

Now, retired after a long career in the telecommunications industry, Kochman coaches sprinters at his son's high school in Upper Darby, Pennsylvania. Ever the competitor, his pride shows through with the achievements of his charges.

"Our team just won the league championship," Kochman says. "For the first time in the history of this league, they won all four relays—an incredible experience."

Kochman's sobering experiences at Penn State—and beyond—could also be called incredible in their own way. So much happened after his days at University Park: a promising pro career aborted by an injury and a life-altering experience surrounding the terrorist attack on 9/11. Now Kochman sometimes has difficulty connecting with the great running back of old that he watches on videotape.

"I ordered the highlight tapes from games when I played there, and I've been looking at them, and I can't even remember when I looked that way or ran that way," Kochman says.

"The incredible thing is, I look at all these highlight films with my son, and they're all black and white. He says, 'Dad, why are they all black and white?' I say, 'Son, we didn't have color then.' My daughter and my son laugh. They show pictures of the clock. It was a ticking clock. No digitals then."

Long before there was a 9/11, in a more innocent time, there were golden days for Kochman racing down the track and running on a football field. He had skipped a grade in grade school and was only 16 when he graduated high school. By then, he had built a reputation as one of Pennsylvania's top schoolboy sprinters and running backs. He starred for Wilkinsburg High in the Pittsburgh suburbs, a 164-pound fullback on an unbeaten high school powerhouse.

At Penn State, he didn't wait long to establish a reputation as one of the school's top running backs. The first time he carried the ball, Kochman went 56 yards for a touchdown.

"I never remembered that until I saw the films," he says. "It was incredible."

That was against West Virginia, midway through Kochman's sophomore season. That same year, Kochman ran back a kickoff 100 yards against Syracuse.

"That was something that probably made my career, as much as anything," Kochman says.

ROGER KOCHMAN

Years lettered: 1959, 1960, 1961 and 1962
Position: Halfback
Accomplishments: Named an All-American halfback
by U.S. Coaches in 1962. That year, he led the Lions in
rushing for the second straight season with 652 yards. He
finished with 1,485 rushing yards for his college career.

He describes the action:

"I remember catching it on the goal line and it was a return up the middle. And when I was going up the middle, all I saw was Syracuse guys."

Suddenly Kochman cut to the right.

"I made it out of desperation because there was no one from Penn State there, and I had to get out of the way. And I made the cut, really behind some tremendous blocks.

"It was bang-bang. Make a block, make a block, cut to the outside—and gone. I could run—I could run very well."

Kochman later figured prominently in Penn State's first Liberty Bowl game, in 1959. In cold, windy conditions in Philadelphia that put a damper on scoring, Kochman scored the only touchdown of the game as the Lions beat Alabama 7-0.

"I scored on a fake field goal," Kochman remembers. "Quarterback Richie Lucas got hurt and Galen Hall took Richie's place. It was the last play of the first half, a screen pass. Galen threw to me and I went in for a touchdown with no time left on the clock."

It wouldn't be the only time that Kochman would hook up with Hall for a key touchdown play in bowl competition. In the 1961 Gator Bowl against Georgia Tech, Kochman caught a TD pass from Hall as the Nittany Lions whipped the Yellowjackets, 30-15. It was literally a blind catch.

"I was running down the sidelines and I looked over my shoulder and I looked right into the sun and didn't see the ball," Kochman recalls. "Galen and I had completed that pass a couple of times earlier in the year, and instinctively, I just put my hands up over my left shoulder, and the ball was there. People don't believe this. . . I literally don't think I saw that ball until it hit my hands."

The Gator Bowl was memorable for another reason, too: he saw the ugly face of racism up close and personal. Dave Robinson was one of Kochman's closest friends. He was also the only African American on the Penn State team. There were incidents in restaurants and hotels barring blacks.

"We went into St. Augustine and the hotel in St. Augustine was the only hotel, I think, in that immediate area where Dave Robinson could stay with us," Kochman says. "And that's the only reason we went there. We actually turned down [another] bowl. That was the era of segregation."

It wasn't the first brush with that sort of thing for the Penn State players, as Kochman recalls.

"I can remember going into West Virginia, and the West Virginia folks referring to Dave with the 'N word.' I can remember going over the fence to go up into the stands and get these people who were screaming these epithets and getting held back by police. You didn't understand segregation until you really experienced it. I think that was a turning point in a lot of our lives where we really understood what segregation was all about."

In 1962, the Nittany Lions went to the Gator Bowl for the second straight season. Even though Kochman thought they had a better team that year, the results didn't show it. The Lions lost to Florida, 17-7.

"That was probably one of the worst situations I've ever been in. There were a number of guys, including myself, who were being recruited actively by pro teams. We just didn't have our heads in the game, and we ended up losing. It was kind of a bummer."

Teams from both the NFL and AFL hoped to sign Kochman. He finally decided on Buffalo of the AFL. His pro career came to a premature end, though, with a knee injury. It was an old story for Kochman, who suffered disabling injuries at various times of his college career. At one point he had to sit out a year.

"It turned out that Buffalo was a great organization," Kochman says. "I got hurt and they took very good care of me. I was really banged up, in the hospital for a very long time. They stuck by me, they paid all the bills. I was fortunate enough to have a guaranteed two-year contract, and they honored it."

After pro football, Kochman went through a couple years of rehab. He then went back to graduate school and got an MBA from Penn State. After graduation, he joined Bell of Pennsylvania, which became Bell Atlantic and later Verizon. He worked with the giant telecommunica-

Roger Kochman, retired after a distinguished career with Verizon, coaches sprinters at his son's high school in Upper Darby, Pennsylvania.
Photo courtesy of Roger Kochman

tions company for nearly 37 years. Kochman became director of security operations in charge of all the physical security for Verizon across the nation. As such, he was responsible for security when contractors came in to restore communications following the World Trade Center disaster on September 11, 2001. Kochman manned the perimeter at Chambers and West Street, the headquarters for emergency management for New York City.

"We had to get a huge number of contractors into 140 West Street, which was adjacent to the Towers. That was the hub of all communications, including Wall Street, in lower Manhattan," Kochman says.

"I had to get our contractors in and make sure they were okay because obviously everyone was concerned about terrorists coming in and wreaking more havoc."

President Bush had issued a mandate to get the stock market back up and working within five days.

"It took thousands of people to get that building back in operation. We did it, and that was an incredible feat."

After retiring from Verizon, Kochman went back to sports to fill out his leisure time. As the coach of his son's sprint team, he applies the same work ethic he learned in high school and at Penn State.

"I tell the guys on the track team: there are probably a hundred guys who can run just as fast as they can, a hundred guys just as big as they are, just as strong as they are.

"And one person is going to separate himself from the pack, because of what they have inside. That's the heart. You can't measure the heart."

Roger Kochman speaks from personal experience

JERRY FARKAS

L ike most football players, Jerry Farkas remembers his first start at Penn State. "It was Boston University and we shut them out, 20-0," Farkas recalls of the September 17, 1960, game at Beaver Stadium. "I had a sack. I always remember those."

But there's another memory, even more vivid and more meaningful, that floods back to the onetime Penn State tackle after more than 40 years away from the game. It was the night that the Nittany Lions displayed the true meaning of the word "team."

The Lions had taken a break from their practice for the 1961 Gator Bowl by going to the movies one night in St. Augustine, Florida. Among them was Dave Robinson, the only black player on the team. An usher ordered Robinson to sit upstairs in the balcony. No blacks were allowed downstairs.

"This was a couple of years after the Civil Rights Act went into effect," Farkas points out.

So what did the Penn State players do? The right thing.

"The entire team went up with Dave to the balcony and watched the movie from there," Farkas says.

It wasn't the only racial incident involving Robinson on that trip.

"But he was quiet about the whole thing," Farkas remembers.

Not so quiet in the game against Georgia Tech, though.

"He was just a demon," Farkas says. "He made a clutch play when Georgia Tech was driving, to not only tackle the quarterback on a rollout, but recover the fumble as well. It was one of those deals where he dove over a blocker in mid-air, hit the quarterback and made him cough up the ball.

"It was just a very athletic play. But I did play next to him and you could just sense all that frustration was coming out in that game, and to his advantage, he channeled it well."

Robinson, who would become a great pro linebacker with the Green Bay Packers, was named the MVP of the game. And Penn State won, 30-15.

The Gator Bowl trip opened the eyes of many of the Penn State players.

"It was a shock to actually experience what a black person would be going through," Farkas says. "To see the signs, 'Colored Drink Here,' or 'Colored Upstairs,' was a real shock.

"I was from the Lehigh Valley area, the cement region. There weren't any blacks in our town. A lot of the players were from the coal region. We weren't around blacks that much, but when we were, it was in an athletic atmosphere, and it didn't matter."

Farkas came out of a solid football program at Northampton High School near Allentown. As a freshman at Penn State, he was given the choice of playing sparingly with the varsity or being red-shirted to give him an extra year of eligibility.

JERRY FARKAS

Years lettered: 1960, 1961 and 1962
Position: Tackle

Jerry Farkas lives in Pennsylvania with his wife, Judi,
following his retirement from the insurance business.
Photo courtesy of Jerry Farkas

"We had three tackles who went on to play in the NFL, and they were seniors, and I wasn't going to be playing before them, so I elected to red-shirt," Farkas says. "It worked out well. I played in every game for three years."

In his first season of action, Farkas played in the 1960 Liberty Bowl against Oregon in snowy Philadelphia. The frigid weather held the crowd down to less than 17,000 in the 100,000-seat Municipal Stadium.

"It was very cold," Farkas says. "In fact, it was funny warming up. This was the old field where Army-Navy used to play all their games. It was a cavernous, old thing, and the wind was blowing, and they painted the field to make it look like grass. Then on the yard markers, I guess they used a combination of lime and something else. It was a thick, gooey substance for the hash marks, and the yard lines. And that stuff was frozen, and it was like jumping over two-by-fours."

No problem for the Lions. They beat the Ducks, 41-12. Farkas played on the "Reddy Team" in Rip Engle's two-team system.

"That's where the balance came in many of those years, especially in the second half," Farkas says. "When you have two teams that can go at it fairly equally, you just wear the other team down and eventually run the ball like you want to in the second half. You control the clock and score points."

Following the victory over Georgia Tech in the 1961 Gator Bowl, the Lions returned to the Gator Bowl in 1962 and were upset by Florida. The loss did not spoil the Penn State experience for Farkas. The Lions record in his three years there: 24-8. Farkas said a "family" feeling existed on the Penn State teams. And it was always "team" first.

"I felt at home and part of the Penn State family," he says.

Following school, Farkas worked as a teacher and coach, first in New Jersey and then Pennsylvania.

"I liked the teaching and the coaching, but it was a tough way to make a go when you're getting paid $4,200 a year," Farkas says.

Especially when you're just married and starting to raise a family. One of Farkas's former teammates got him into the insurance business with State Farm in Lebanon, Pennsylvania. He spent more than 36 years with the insurance giant before retiring as a manager.

Farkas still keeps in touch with his old Penn State buddies. The Football Lettermen's Club makes it easy.

"We have over a thousand members," boasts Farkas, who has three children with his wife, Judi. "Many have season tickets, or some come back for occasional games."

There's always a meeting place in the Letterman's Lot next to Beaver Stadium.

"You just kind of gravitate to different areas of the lot based on the years you played. And if you're going to find your teammates, they're going to be there, and at the Lettermen's Lounge in the Stadium. It's just a way of perpetuating these friendships."

For Farkas, nothing's changed at Penn State over the years.

"It really is one huge family, and there is a relative closeness about it all, even though the numbers are so great in terms of the size of the school and the number of players over the years," Farkas says.

Once a Penn State man, always a Penn State man.

CHUCK SIEMINSKI

When the Soviets were beaten by the Americans in the 1980 Lake Placid Olympics, it was called the "Miracle on Ice." When a group of college football players beat the world-champion Green Bay Packers in 1963, it was a miracle on grass.

Three Penn State players helped to pull off the shocking upset in the annual game in Chicago matching the College All-Stars against the NFL champions. Chuck Sieminski was one of them.

"It was the last time the college all-stars ever beat the pros," remembers Sieminski, a tackle who played at Penn State in the early '60s. "To Vince Lombardi, it was the worst defeat of his life, losing to the college all-stars."

Accompanying Sieminski to Chicago from Penn State were Roger Kochman and Dave Robinson.

"They were pushing all three of us for All-American in 1962," Sieminski recalls.

All three were drafted by the pros, and all of them had different stories to tell in their NFL lives. But this is Sieminski's story, and how he got from Penn State to the pros.

"It was the era at the time that Penn State made a decision to go big time," Sieminski recalls of his time at Penn State from 1960-62. "We played in four straight bowl games."

Sieminski played in three of them—the 1960 Liberty Bowl and the 1961 and 1962 Gator Bowls. As a freshman he was redshirted, but did get to travel with the Lions for the first Liberty Bowl game in 1959.

"They had two tackles then, Chuck Janerrette, and Andy Stynchula," Sieminski says, explaining why he wasn't starting. "Back in those days, you played both ways. The next three years, I started.

"Your freshman year, you had your own schedule. We had four freshman games: Army, Navy, West Virginia and Pitt. Then after our season ended, we would run the foreign offense, or defense, on Monday for the varsity, whatever they were practicing at the time."

In his three years as a starter, Penn State went 7-3, 8-3 and 9-2, and won two of three bowl games. In the second bowl game, not too many people gave Penn State a chance to beat Georgia Tech in the Gator Bowl in Jacksonville, Florida. So guess what? Penn State won, 30-15.

"Bobby Dodds's teams were very highly ranked," Sieminski says. "They were a little disappointed that they were playing Penn State. But that was a big stepping stone in our recruiting as well as making that transition to another level in Penn State history."

CHUCK SIEMINSKI

Years lettered: 1960, 1961 and 1962
Position: Tackle
Accomplishments: Played for the College
All-Stars in an exhibition game against the
NFL champion Green Bay Packers in 1963.

Not that there was a big budget for football, like there is today. Sieminski remembers times on the road when the team would be lodged in a forestry camp.

"There was no heat. There would be bunk beds there and it was near a lake. All the crickets and frogs were croaking and snoring. None of the coaches would stay there. They used to drive us out and give us a sandwich and an apple and milk. One of the trainers probably stayed . . . but they bunked us down. Nobody got very much sleep. They saved a lot of money, but at the same time we didn't get much sleep."

In 1962, a three-point loss to Army was the only blemish on Penn State's record.

"We were ranked third in the nation, undefeated, and we lost to Army on a busted play, a fake field goal that went awry, and they scored on it," Siemenski recalls of the 9-6 loss at West Point.

The Nittany Lions then beat Syracuse, California, Maryland, West Virginia, Holy Cross and Pittsburgh. Ranked No. 9 in the country, they accepted another invitation to the Gator Bowl. Their opponent: Florida, which many of the Penn State players deemed an unworthy opponent.

"At the time Penn State accepted the invitation, Florida was 6 and 4. We were 9 and 1 at the time. The Gator Bowl committee wanted to have a Florida team in the Gator Bowl.

"We made a commitment. We were thinking Florida would win their last [regular-season] game and finish 7-4, but they ended up losing it. All of a sudden, they were 6-5 and now we're 9-1. This was their whole season. We were down psychologically playing a team with that record."

That wasn't the only thing bothering the Penn State players, as Siemenski remembers. The Nittany Lions featured Robinson, a black player, and southern hospitality was scarce in Florida for African Americans at the time. One day after practice, Sieminski, Robinson and another player stopped at a soda fountain. They all ordered Cokes.

Sieminski remembers: "They gave me and this guy a glass of Coke and they gave Dave an empty glass and turned it upside down. He said, 'We don't serve blacks here.' And we just left our dime, and left our soda, and all three of us walked out. That was one of our first experiences of what it was like in those days."

The atmosphere didn't bode well for a good Penn State showing, and the result was a 17-7 loss to Florida. A better showing for Sieminski and a couple of his Penn State buddies in the All-Star Game against the Packers took away some of the pain from that Gator Bowl loss. Robinson would go on to a brilliant pro career with the Packers. Kochman also was headed for stardom in the pros, but his career was cut short by injury in an NFL game. Sieminski, meanwhile, was picked by pro teams in two leagues, Boston of the American Football League and San Francisco of the National Football League. But he had a red-shirt year remaining in college.

"I decided to go back to Penn State for another year's playing experience before going into the pros," he says.

He eventually joined the 49ers of the NFL. He played three years in San Francisco before moving to the Atlanta Falcons. He later played for Detroit and Philadelphia.

"With the Eagles, I went through training camp and was released, the last cut before the start of the season," he says. "I was told by the defensive coach it was for economic reasons. They went with a younger player for less money. I was very fortunate, I had six years in, and I always say seven, because when you go through training camp, it's like another season."

His pro football career behind him, Sieminski went back to school for a master's degree. He entered the education system in Pennsylvania, teaching and coaching football at the high school level. For a while, he worked with his brother, who was a coach in Hazleton, Pennsylvania. He also served as president of his school district for 12 years "and just enjoyed raising my children." He and his wife, Barbara, have four children and five grandchildren.

Sieminski, who was recently accepted into the Pennsylvania Sports Hall of Fame, is now retired. He loves spending time traveling and visiting his grandchildren.

He can always tell them stories about his football days. After all, he isn't short on those.

PETE LISKE

"We're having a lot of fun with the baseball program and doing well," Pete Liske says cheerily from his office at Penn State.

Once a record-breaking Penn State quarterback and later a successful pro player, Liske is on the offense once more these days. He's employed as the director for major gifts for intercollegiate athletics at Penn State. One of his primary goals these days: Build a new baseball stadium and bring a minor league team to State College.

"A team will do exceptionally well here, because there's not a lot of other activity here in the summer time," Liske says. "You have a lot of retirees coming back. It will be a perfect setting for minor league clubs, and it will certainly help the college team, too."

Liske brought plenty of business experience to the job when he first came back to Penn State in the fall of 2001. At the University of Washington, he was the associate athletic director in charge of development, marketing and promotions. He also served as athletic director at the University of Idaho and the University of Toledo.

In a varied career after football, Liske was also a businessman and a back judge in the NFL. He was living in Boulder, Colorado, at the time when he first got back into football.

"I started officiating because I wanted to stay involved in some kind of athletics. I knew officiating would do it," Liske says. "And I ended up officiating in the NFL for six or seven years."

Liske also found work officiating games in the Western Athletic Conference.

"I just realized that I was really looking forward much more to the weekends than anything else, and that I missed athletics," says Liske. "So I wanted to get back into it full time, and decided that administration would be the place that I could maybe do some things."

After stints at Washington, Idaho and Toledo, Liske came back to Penn State "to finish things out in athletic administration." Thus Liske completed the full circle back to Penn State following his exciting years as a football and baseball player at State College. In football, he led the Lions in passing in 1962 and 1963 and played in two bowl games. In baseball, he led the Lions to the College World Series.

Liske was one of many football players recruited then by Joe Paterno out of New Jersey. Paterno was the offensive coach under Rip Engle.

"He was very intense, very competitive," Liske says of Paterno. "He really had that attitude—'Eastern football doesn't take a back seat to anyone.' That was one of his big mantras at that time, that Penn State needs to stake its claim as a university and certainly as a football program, too."

PETE LISKE

Years lettered: 1961, 1962 and 1963
Position: Quarterback
Accomplishments: Led the team in passing in both 1962
(1,037 yards) and 1963 (1,117). In 1962, received the
Coogan Award as the best player in the Penn State-Pitt game.

It was already starting to do that, with a 7-0 victory over Alabama in the 1959 Liberty Bowl—Penn State's first bowl victory. It continued with a 41-12 beating of Oregon in the second Liberty Bowl, in 1960.

By the time Liske was making his presence felt on the Penn State team, the Lions made two more bowl visits to complete a run of four straight under Engle.

Penn State's schedule in the '60s was taking on more of a national look with games against California, Oregon, Air Force, Rice, Missouri, Miami, Illinois, UCLA and Ohio State.

"We were trying to stretch a little bit and get some national recognition for the program, and probably even more so for Eastern football at that time," Liske says. "It wasn't just for Penn State. The schools in the East really weren't getting much respect from the rest of the country."

After losing in the 1962 Gator Bowl to Florida, Liske returned for his senior season and was greeted with brighter moments. The first game of the season against Oregon comes to mind. Then Liske set a Penn State completion percentage record, one that still stands. He completed 11 of 12 passes, for a 91.7 completion rate, as the Nittany Lions beat Oregon, 17-7. Later in the season Liske completed 14 of 24 passes for 168 yards and a touchdown to lead the Lions to a 10-7 upset victory over Ohio State. Liske didn't let a huge hostile crowd of 83,519 at Ohio Stadium affect his focus.

"They were ranked No. 1, and they were undefeated going into it," Liske says. "It was really just a case of us wanting to play a Big Ten school, a nationally ranked school, and we thought we could play with them."

When Liske graduated, he left school with six Penn State records.

"I didn't have to grow up for a while because I could play football for about another 12 years," says Liske, who came back to school in the off season to get an MBA while playing professionally.

He played briefly with the New York Jets, and then went to Canada and became a star in the Canadian Football League. In 1967, he passed for 40 touchdowns and won the CFL's Outstanding Player of the Year award.

"We had had some successes and some struggles," Liske says, speaking collectively. "We had a whole bunch of records up there that Doug Flutie finally came along and beat. That was fun."

He had more fun when he came back to the States to play for the Denver Broncos of the American Football League. Liske remembered one particular day against the Jets, his former team. Replacing injured Steve Tensi at quarterback, Liske rallied the Broncos to three touchdowns as they beat the Jets, 21-19.

How sweet it was for Liske.

"The Jets had just won the Super Bowl the year before," Liske remembers. "A lot of the players were still on the team. So it was kind of nice to be able to beat them after getting traded from New York."

Liske played another season in Denver and then two more in Philadelphia before retiring and starting on a business career and the long, winding road that took him back to Penn State.

"I thought I could come back to my alma mater and do some things for the program, to kind of help out," Liske says.

So far, so good.

ED
STEWART

Ed Stewart has stories to tell. Stories about the toughest football player he ever knew, and the most "surreal" game he ever played in. Of course, there are Joe Paterno stories, too. Everyone cracks up when they hear the "Three Mothers" story. Even Joe likes to tell it once in a while.

First, Stewart's "greatest" thrill at Penn State.

"I'll tell you what, there was no thrill like coming out of that tunnel at Beaver Stadium," recalls Stewart, who played line positions on both sides of the ball in the 1960s. "Of course, everybody gets goose bumps when they come out. But I can remember it felt like I was almost floating coming out on the field."

When Stewart played in the mid-'60s, Beaver Stadium was about half the size that it is now. Maybe they could get 49,000 to 50,000 in there if the fire marshal was looking the other way.

"We set an attendance record every year we were there, and I think that was just an early indication of how popular Penn State football was going to become," says Stewart, now retired after working many years in the corporate world as an auditor.

The son of a steelworker, Stewart grew up in the western Pennsylvania town of Beaver. The area was known for turning out great football talent. Joe Namath, for one, came out of nearby Beaver Falls.

Stewart was excited when he, two buddies and their mothers all drove up to State College on a visit to see Paterno in his senior year of high school.

"Joe remembers that visit," Stewart says. "He'll still talk about that recruiting story with those three moms."

At the time, Paterno was dating a Penn State student named Sue who would eventually be his wife. That brought Stewart to the "Three Mothers" story:

"Of course the mothers were in love with Paterno. He was the assistant coach and very charming. He's a great recruiter. But he was dating Sue at the time. Sue is quite a few years younger than Joe, and our mothers actually gave Joe a hard time about dating such a young lady. One of them—we were all with her when she said it—said 'I hope your intentions are honorable.' And we're going, 'Hey, hey, hey, we want to come to school here, don't say stuff like that.'"

An article in the paper that announced that Joe and Sue had gotten engaged reassured the mothers.

When Stewart played at Penn State, Glenn Ressler was the biggest star. In 1964, Ressler made All-America as a middle guard and center. He would go on to become an

ED STEWART

Years lettered: 1963, 1964 and 1965
Position: Defensive tackle

All-Pro guard with Baltimore in the National Football League. Ressler gets Stewart's vote as the most impressive player he saw in his time.

"Glenn was the old school," remembers Stewart. "He never lifted a weight or anything, but this guy was the strongest person I had ever seen in my life. He was like a bulldozer. He could just push anybody, or block anybody, off the field and he was really, really tough on defense.

"I scrimmaged against him a lot, and people ask me, 'Who's the best player you ever played against?' and I'll tell them, 'Glenn Ressler.' And they ask, 'Who did he play for?' And I'd say, 'Penn State.' They'd say, 'Well, that doesn't count.' And I'd say, 'Yeah, it does, because I played against him more than anybody, and he was the toughest guy I ever played against.'"

In 1963, Penn State went to Columbus and shocked Ohio State with a 10-7 victory. That set up a "revenge" motive for the Buckeyes in 1964. The Lions had lost their first three games and were 3-4 when they traveled to Columbus to meet Ohio State, which was unbeaten and ranked No. 2 in the country.

"We were struggling, but we were playing better," Stewart says. "We knew we had a good team, we just hadn't really put it all together. And so we went out there, and all the papers were talking about was the fact that Ohio State had a revenge factor because we had beaten them the year before, and we shouldn't have. And this year was payback time."

But the Lions had watched films on Ohio State and felt they could beat the Buckeyes.

"We went into Ohio Stadium—there were something like 86,000 people there—and it was the most surreal football game I had ever played in," recalls Stewart. "I was the starting defensive tackle, and I knew we were controlling everything. We had a lead at halftime, and it was three and out for them on every play in that half, except for one series where they quick-kicked and had a two and out.

"And so the defense didn't have a lot of plays. But we went in at halftime, and they used to line us up on benches at that time. They put all the offensive starters on the first bench, like a classroom setting almost, and the defensive guys were all on the second bench. We had our white uniforms on because we were away."

John Deibert, the other defensive tackle, was sitting next to Stewart.

"He whispered to me, 'Ed, how many plays did you have?' I didn't know. I was sitting there, trying to count them up, but I was thinking, okay, I had these plays, and then I was on the kickoff team, and I can't remember, I had something like 12 or 13 plays. He said, 'I only had eight.'

"And we were sitting there, and I'm looking at John and myself, and all the other defensive guys, I was kind of looking up and down the row, and our white uniforms were still completely white. It looked like we hadn't even gone on the field yet. The offensive guys were sitting in front of us, and their uniforms were so dirty you could hardly read the numbers because they had been on the field the whole half.

"And I thought, Oh, my God, I said to John, 'Look at their uniforms and look at our uniforms,' and of course, they were filthy and we were almost spotless. I couldn't believe it. We kept thinking, it will change in the third quarter. We'll go out, and it's going to get a lot tougher, and it didn't. We went out and just kept it going."

In one of the greatest performances ever by a Penn State team, the Lions routed the heavily favored Buckeyes, 27-0.

Stewart's last college season in 1965 was also the last for head coach Rip Engle, who gave way to Paterno.

"It was the best four years of my life," Stewart says. "I had a good time, made a lot of good friends, and the experience overall was really enjoyable."

An accounting major, Stewart didn't have any problems finding work in the field. He eventually became a CPA while raising two sons with his wife, Janis.

"I know that Penn State football helped me get in the door of several places," Stewart says.

In 1980, Stewart took over the internal audit staff of a Pennsylvania gas company and ran it for 20 years until the company was bought out. Since retired, Stewart reflects on the impact that Penn State football has had on his life.

"I think a lot of my management style, if that's what you want to call it, was based on my football experiences, in trying to find people and put them in a position to do good work," Stewart says.

Just like the Penn State coaching staff did for Stewart.

JOHN SLADKI

Johnstown, Pennsylvania, in the 1960s was Steeltown, USA. And football was life. "Friday night, Saturday night, football was the big thing in town," says John Sladki, a defensive back for Penn State from 1965-66. "Football was in my blood."

Sladki remembers when times were good for high school football in Johnstown and other western Pennsylvania towns in the '50s and '60s. They would fill a 12,000-seat stadium for a high school football game. That all changed when the steel mills began shutting down.

"The mills died. The towns died. The sports died. And people just moved on," Sladki recalls. "They're products of some other area now."

Before things changed, the region did produce some of football's most glamorous names: Joe Montana, Joe Namath, Jim Kelly and Jack Ham, to name a few.

Sladki played quarterback on a powerful Johnstown High School team.

"Nobody wanted to play us. We had to go all over the place just to get our 10-game schedule in."

Sladki also played basketball at Johnstown High. But when it came to picking a sport for college, football was his first—and only—choice.

"There was no doubt in my mind. I loved basketball, but football was the way to go," Sladki says.

Sladki went from fast times at Johnstown High to hard times at Penn State. He was in the middle of a difficult transition at University Park, playing in Rip Engle's last season and then Joe Paterno's first as head coach.

The Nittany Lions closed out the Engle Era with a 5-5 record in 1965. Paterno, Engle's assistant for 16 years, struggled through another 5-5 season in 1966.

"I think Joe probably was trying to find his own identity," says Sladki.

So was Sladki. He was recruited as a quarterback and wound up playing in the defensive backfield once he made the varsity as a sophomore. On the freshman team, Sladki actually played both ways in the era before specialization.

JOHN SLADKI

Years lettered: 1965 and 1966
Position: Defensive backfield

"Then in my sophomore year, they said, there's an offense, there's a defense, and you choose one or the other."

The Penn State coaches actually made Sladki's choice for him.

"I ended up playing in the secondary," Sladki recalls.

Sladki remembers an aggressive, young Paterno.

"He got involved in everything. Paterno would come around to each individual drill. He had the knowledge of what the linemen were doing, he had the knowledge of the backs and he had knowledge of the passing game."

The schedule maker didn't do Paterno any favors in his first year. There were no breathers on a schedule that included Michigan State, the eventual co-national champion with Notre Dame, and UCLA and Georgia Tech, both ranked in the Top Five when Penn State played them.

"I guess that's not the way to get baptized." Sladki says.

But Sladki had the greatest respect for Paterno's coaching skills. JoePa would soon prove his worth with some extraordinary teams in the late '60s, and beyond.

Due to a knee injury in his freshman year, Sladki was redshirted. He sat out his sophomore year before finally seeing action in some memorable games during his junior and senior years. One in 1965, however, he would like to forget.

"We were playing California out at California," Sladki recalls. "There was one second to go and we were up. The quarterback launched a pass in my area, and the receiver behind me pushed me."

"When you get pushed in the back, you bow a little bit, and the ball went off my fingertips and [the California receiver] caught it in the end zone and they won."

The referee never called a penalty against the Cal receiver who pushed Sladki. And Sladki remembered a long flight home from California after that 21-17 loss. He also remembered one of his teammates making a private confession to him.

"The defensive end in front of me on that play said, 'John, I'm not going to admit this to anybody, but the ball went off my fingers before it went off your fingers.' He didn't want to tell anybody, because he didn't want to take the blame for it."

Sladki had a more positive experience in 1966 when he intercepted passes against Pitt to help the Nittany Lions beat their longtime intrastate rivals, 48-24.

"That was nice," Sladki says. "That was a big rivalry because we were independent then."

It was also a redemption game for Sladki, making up for a loss to Pitt in the previous season. Turned out, the victory over Pitt was Sladki's last game at Penn State. Although he still had a year of eligibility left, he decided to hang up his cleats. But he wasn't entirely finished with sports. Following graduation, he returned to Johnstown to teach and coach football and basketball at his old high school.

"I majored in accounting at Penn State, and I loved sports so much that I decided to get into coaching," he says. "I was able to go back and get my education degree, because I wanted to coach. I just wanted to be a part of Johnstown because it was like my bloodline."

Naturally, Sladki adapted some of the things he had learned at Penn State to his coaching work at Johnstown.

John Sladki is a retired teacher living with his wife, Gina, in Johnstown, Pennsylvania. He works part-time painting and remodeling houses.
Photo courtesy of John Sladki

"When I went to coach at Johnstown, I was all into techniques and drills. Individual techniques and drills win ballgames. You just don't go out and do group work. We spent many, many hours working on individual techniques, and I think that's what wins football games."

Meanwhile, Sladki taught for 34 years in Johnstown High's business department before retiring. He's currently doing part-time work painting and remodeling houses.

And constantly being reminded about his years as a Penn State football player.

"It really means a lot to you after you graduate," Sladki says. "I'd see my friends and they would say, 'John played at Penn State.' That makes you feel good, to be part of something. And that's your identity."

CHARLIE PITTMAN

"We're living proof that the Grand Experiment works," says Charles Pittman, referring to himself and his son, Tony.

In the '60s, Pittman was Joe Paterno's first All-America running back. At the time, he was known less formally as "Charlie." From 1967-69 he led the Nittany Lions in rushing for three straight seasons—2,236 career yards and 30 touchdowns in all.

"I was in [Paterno's] first class," Pittman proudly points out. "If they don't get me, they don't get Franco [Harris] and Lydell [Mitchell]. I'm not the best who ever played there, but I opened the door for a lot of guys behind me."

His story doesn't end there. Fast forward to the 90s. Tony Pittman was blossoming into an outstanding cornerback for the Lions.

Like father, like son.

"We have so many similarities," Charles Pittman says. "We both played on undefeated, untied teams. We both never lost a game when we played there. We both were academic All-Americans. We come from different generations . . . and we're quite often asked what's it like to play for Joe Paterno."

So, what's it like?

"Joe Paterno had a real knack for judging talent and putting people in the right positions. But he also knew how to manage his personnel emotionally.

"I remember him coming in before almost every game, putting his arm on my shoulder and saying, 'Charlie, we need you today. We need a big run out of you, we need a big play out of you today.'"

Pittman recalls the time Penn State played Missouri in the Orange Bowl on January 1, 1970.

"The playing conditions were horrendous, the humidity was just stifling, so we went in at halftime, and they were discussing strategy for the second half.

"I just stripped, laid down on the bench. I needed my energy and my strength, and Joe came over to me and said, 'Charlie, we need you in the second half. We're counting on you. I said, 'Joe, I'll be there—don't worry. I will be there.'

"And he walked away and let me go. I like that about him, because he knew how to motivate individually. Team-wise, too, he could do that, but individually he knew what it took to get certain individuals going, and he always let me know I was needed."

The results speak for themselves. Against Missouri, Pittman was Penn State's leading rusher with 83 yards. Plus he caught two passes for 10 more, as the Nittany Lions won, 10-3.

Then there was the 1967 Gator Bowl against Florida State.

CHARLIE PITTMAN

Years lettered: 1967, 1968 and 1969
Position: Running back
Accomplishments: Led the Lions in rushing for three straight seasons. He amassed 2,236 yards and 30 touchdowns for hiscareer and was named an All-American in 1969. He was also named an academic All-American.

"Back then there weren't too many black players who played in the Gator Bowl, it was a pretty hostile environment," Pittman recalls. "And [Paterno] came over to me and said before we went down there, 'You get a chance to show a national TV audience how good you really are. It's going to be pretty hostile down there, but just show them how good you really are on national TV.'

"So all during the time we were practicing, I kept that in the back of my mind. I remember before the game, they had us in a tent outside of the field, and the spectators were beating up on the tent. They were going wild, they were trying to get us through the tent. Then they played the national anthem, it was kind of quiet, and then they played Dixie, and the whole stadium erupted. I thought, 'What in the world am I doing down here?'"

Then Penn State took the field, and things got wilder.

"They start booing us. That entire game, [Florida State players] were calling me names, trying to pull my eyes out, hitting me on the bottom of the pile, but I just kept my cool, kept my poise. I just remembered what Joe said, 'Show a national TV audience how good you really are.' That's what I tried to do."

Show them he did: Pittman led all rushers with 124 yards.

The story most told about Pittman: He had been a celebrated high school player in Maryland, but at first wasn't having an easy time of it at Penn State.

"I had come through what I thought was a great spring practice. I came out and I was a third-team back," Pittman says. "We opened against Navy in my home state and there I was, on the bench. I was the star running back coming out of Maryland and I didn't get on the field. And when I did get on the field, there was no attempt to ever get me the ball. I was very disillusioned."

One day Pittman was in the locker room when Paterno walked in with an NFL scout.

"Joe asked me, 'Well, how did you do in the freshman game this week?' I said, 'I only carried the ball two times for 14 yards.' And he said, 'Well, the next time someone asks you, tell them you averaged seven yards a carry.' That's putting a positive spin on things. When he said that, my head came up, and then I heard him turn to the guy and say, 'That's the guy that's going to make me a great football coach.'"

Neither coach nor player could envision the kind of success Penn State would have in the three-year period when Pittman played there—three bowl visits and two perfect seasons, in 1968 and 1969. Paterno and his "Grand Experiment," which emphasized the student athlete, was starting to pay off.

Pittman was an important part of the puzzle. Before coming to Penn State, he had set the Maryland high school scoring record while playing at Edmonton High School in Baltimore. But when it came time for his decision on a college, he was having a difficult time.

"My idol at the time was number 24, Lenny Moore for the Baltimore Colts," recalls Pittman. "In the year that I set the scoring record in Maryland, Lenny set the touchdown record in the National Football League. I think he had 26 touchdowns in that one year.

"He had gone to Penn State and he had played for the Colts. So naturally, that's what I wanted to do . . . go to Penn State and sort of follow Lenny Moore's career."

At the same time, the University of Maryland was also recruiting Pittman.

"Lou Saban took over as head coach of Maryland. And that was my home state, so I was torn whether I wanted to stay home and play in my home state or go to Penn State and follow in the footsteps of my football idol."

Saban inadvertently helped Pittman make up his mind.

"Saban said to me, 'Well, if you go to Penn State, do you think you could start as a sophomore?' Back in those days, freshman couldn't play. 'But if you come to Maryland, I can guarantee you can start as a sophomore.'

"In reality, what he did, he questioned my ability. You know, you say I'm good enough to start here, but not good enough to start at Penn State. That was a challenge that I liked. I'll show you: I'll go to Penn State and I'll start as a sophomore! And that's how I made my decision to go to Penn State."

For a while, he wasn't so sure he had made the right choice. Despite his great high school credentials, Pittman didn't play much at first—unless you count playing in practice against the varsity. But he promised himself, and his parents, that he would start as a sophomore.

Following that Maryland game in which he only received a couple touches, the odds didn't shift in Pittman's favor. He got in for a few plays in the next game against Miami but never touched the ball. Pittman had guaranteed his parents that he would be starting by the third game. But it didn't look like a promise he could keep.

"And then the third game came, we played UCLA," Pittman remembers. "Bob Campbell had a great game, but he got hurt in the first half and couldn't play anymore, so I had to start the second half. So I missed my prediction by half a game. And then after that, I started every game."

Penn State lost to UCLA 17-15, but Pittman never experienced defeat again as a starter for the Nittany Lions. He was one of a talented group of sophomores inserted into the lineup en masse the following week.

"Joe Paterno took [the upper-classmen] out and put us in," Pittman remembers. "Paterno said, 'Okay—I'm going with my sophomores.' He put everybody in: [Jim] Kates and [Dennis] Onkotz and Neal Smith and Pete Johnson and me . . . he started all of us. It was probably one of the best decisions he ever made."

The Nittany Lions started winning and didn't stop for three seasons. By the time their unbeaten streak ended in 1970, Penn State had gone a school record 31 games without a loss.

"I don't think the first year we thought we could be a dynasty, but we thought we were pretty good," Pittman says. "We were just a smart, quick team, and one of the worst things Paterno could say in practice was, 'Okay, blue against blue.' That meant the first-team offense had to go against the first-team defense.

"I used to dread that, because that's how good they were. But if we could move the ball on them, we felt we could move it against anybody in the country."

And often they did. In Pittman's senior year, when he shared the backfield with Mitchell and Harris, Penn State had one of the top offensive lines in the country. It featured Dave Joyner, Dave Bradley, John Kulka, Rick Buzin and Bill Lenkaitis.

The best team that Pittman played on? Probably 1969, he thinks.

"We were a year older and we had Franco and we had Lydell," Pittman says. "A couple games we had 100 yards each. Franco was tough inside. Lydell was tough. And I had the speed on the outside. We were a pretty good football team. And in my senior year, we only had three turnovers the whole season."

After the season, Paterno advised Pittman to go to Harvard Business School. But Pittman wasn't thinking MBA; he was thinking NFL.

"As I played more and more, I got a little better and a little better," he says. "I thought I owed the NFL a chance. If I didn't, there would always be doubt as to whether I was good enough to play there."

The NFL was not all that Pittman expected.

"I felt like Jim Ryan, the great miler. He didn't know how to come in second. Rather than come in second, he would walk off the track. And I didn't know how to be a second teamer, or come off the bench. So I didn't perform well in the National Football League at all, even though during scrimmages and things like that I felt I played well."

A little while later, Pittman ran into Paterno at a banquet. The coach had the same advice he had before: forget about football and get on with your life. Pittman did just that, after an abbreviated three-year career in the NFL.

"When he said that to me, he really made me want to get on with my life, because I didn't go to college to be an NFL player in the first place," Pittman says. "So why was I chasing a dream that I didn't really want? It wasn't my dream.

Charlie Pittman, based in South Bend, Indiana, manages a group of newspapers for Schurz Communications.
Photo courtesy of Charlie Pittman

"I went there to be the first one in my family to graduate from college and to do something with my brain."

While he didn't go to Harvard, he took classes at Gannon College in Erie.

"It propelled me in my professional career today. It got me moving in the right direction."

Pittman was first a banker, then got into the newspaper business in Erie, Pennsylvania. For 10 years he did just about everything—even wrote a sports column. He moved to the *Charlotte Observer* in North Carolina, where he trained to be a publisher. That eventually led him to his present position as senior vice president of newspapers at Schurz Communications. Based in South Bend, Indiana, Pittman has the responsibility of managing 10 daily and three weekly newspapers.

"It's a great business. I really love what I do," says Pittman, who has a son and two daughters with his wife, Maurese.

A star at Penn State, and a star in business. It's where Pittman has always belonged—on the first team.

TED
KWALICK

"I'll tell you what's had an impact on my life," Ted Kwalick says by phone from California, "I have a 12-year-old who plays volleyball, and I do not miss her tournaments. Business and everything else comes second.

"When I was a kid, there were no sports for girls, and it's such a great thing. And to see her passion for it, she just loves what she does. Hopefully she got some of that from me. She has a great work ethic and it's just a pleasure to watch her."

The same could be said about Kwalick when he was an All-American receiver at Penn State and then an All-Pro pass catcher in the NFL. Now a father of four girls, including rising volleyball star Noelle, Kwalick fondly recalls his gridiron days—particularly his days at Penn State.

"I couldn't have been happier with my college experience," Kwalick says. "It was great going to Penn State, having that whole ambience of being in Happy Valley and Joe Paterno being the head coach.

"Joe stressed there's more to life than football. The things I learned from that football experience carried me through a lot of hard times in life."

Playing from 1966-68, Kwalick was in the middle of an evolution that produced the first of Paterno's great teams and raised the bar for Penn State football. Kwalick also was in the middle of an evolution in the sport of football itself.

"The position of tight end was just coming into fruition at that time," Kwalick recalls.

In the pros, the tight end was used as both a blocker and a receiver. But he was usually only used as a pass catcher in short yardage situations. Kwalick added the element of the "deep threat." Here were two players in one—a big, durable receiver to get needed short yardage and also speedy enough to break a long one like a wide receiver. One NFL scout said Kwalick ran like a halfback after he caught the ball. And, at six-foot-four, 225 pounds, Kwalick was tough to tackle in the open field.

One defining moment in his Penn State career: Against Syracuse in 1967, Kwalick caught a pass over the middle. He bounced off a tackler, evaded two more and raced 30 yards until he was finally stopped. And it took no less than three defenders to bring him down!

Kwalick also led the way as a blocker. He cleared paths for Charlie Pittman as the Nittany Lions went to a run-oriented offense in the unbeaten season of 1968. Considering the conservative nature of that offense, Kwalick still managed to catch 31 passes for 403 yards. His all-around contributions were recognized in the Heisman Trophy race, where Kwalick finished fourth.

TED KWALICK

Years lettered: 1966, 1967 and 1968
Position: Tight end
Accomplishments: Two-time All-American and a member of
the College Football Hall of Fame. In his college career,
caught 86 passes for 1,343 yards and 10 TDs. As a senior,
finished fourth in the Heisman Trophy voting. Considered
a special player who revolutionized the tight end position.

All in all, Kwalick's college career statistics were impressive for a tight end that blocked as much as he caught passes. In three years, he caught 86 passes for 1,343 yards and 10 touchdowns. He was named to the All-America team in 1967 and 1968. As such, he was Paterno's first All-America player and the first two-time All-American in Penn State history.

His final game at Penn State was one of his most memorable: Against Kansas in the Orange Bowl, Kwalick caught six passes for 74 yards. It was one of the legendary games in Penn State history.

Trailing 14-7 with 1:16 left, the Lions were on the 50-yard line. Suddenly they were on the 3 after a 47-yard pass from Chuck Burkhart to Bob Campbell. Then they were in the end zone on a rollout by Burkhart. It was now Kansas 14, Penn State 13.

The Lions went for the two-point conversion.

"They called a pass play and Chuck Burkhart threw it in the end zone, and there were about three guys on me and it went over my head," Kwalick remembers.

Game over. The Jayhawks and their fans were celebrating. But hold on—Kansas was penalized for having 12 men on the field. That gave Penn State another crack at the two-pointer.

"We called a running play and I was blocking John Zook," Kwalick said. "Bobby Campbell got the ball and I was lucky enough to get a decent block on John, and Bobby got in the end zone."

Final: Penn State 15, Kansas 14. The victory preserved a perfect season for Penn State at 11-0. The Nittany Lions finished No. 2 in the national polls and were on their way to greater glories.

Kwalick would later become an All-Pro, playing for San Francisco and Oakland—with a short stay in the World Football League. At Oakland, he won a Super Bowl.

Kwalick had no such soaring aspirations when he first decided to go to Penn State.

"My whole goal was just to get a college education and be a high school football coach and teach physical education," Kwalick says.

At Montour High School in McKees Rocks, outside of Pittsburgh, Kwalick was his school's first All-American.

Penn State was his first choice because of the educational commitment to athletes.

"It was kind of ironic because my mother has 14 kids on her side of the family, and I was the first one out of all the nephews and nieces to ever go to college."

Rip Engle, who was still Penn State's head coach in 1965, recruited Kwalick. Unbeknownst to Kwalick, it was going to be Engle's final season, and Paterno would be taking over in 1966. That was Kwalick's sophomore year, and his first varsity experience.

"Joe didn't know where he wanted to play me," Kwalick remembers.

Finally, he settled on Kwalick as a tight end, basically the same position he had played in high school. After a 5-5 season in 1966, Penn State went 8-2-1 in 1967 and played in the Gator Bowl against Florida State.

"It was Joe's first bowl game. Joe at that point of his career was so paranoid he changed the whole offense. He put me at flanker, because back then he was concerned. He had sent films of the whole season [to Florida State] and Joe was so paranoid that people would pick up stuff.

*Ted Kwalick, a father of four girls, currently
runs a power conditioning firm in California.*
Photo courtesy of Ted Kwalick

"He would change the offense around almost on a weekly basis. You had to really be on top of your mental game, because he'd change a lot of things around and put in new things."

It's hard to say whether Paterno's player switches did any good, but Penn State did come out with a 17-17 tie against Florida State.

Then came the 1968 team and a splendid group of players. Kwalick, Pittman and Burkhart were the high-profile players on offense. The defense featured Denny Onkotz, Jack Ham, Steve Smear, Mike Reid and Pete Johnson.

"I feel honored to be Joe's first All-American, but that wasn't really the key," says Kwalick. "What we did as a team was so critical. We started out my sophomore year, we were 5-5, and then my junior year, 8-2-1. And then my senior year I think we had the best college defense in the country."

The only close game the Nittany Lions had during the regular season was against Army. Kwalick remembered that one especially, and for a good reason.

"Army came back and almost beat us," Kwalick says. "They kicked an onside kick and Dave Bradley jumped on it, and one of the Cadets punched it out of his leg and popped it into my hands, I was lucky enough to run down the sidelines and score. That put the game out of reach."

Penn State prevailed, 28-24, and finished out the season with wins over Miami, Maryland, Pittsburgh, Syracuse and Kansas.

The next year, Kwalick was playing his football in the pros with the San Francisco 49ers, who made him their number one draft pick in 1969. With the Niners, he eventually became an All-Pro in 1972, 1973 and 1974. Kwalick spent some time in the ill-fated World Football League before signing as a free agent with the Oakland Raiders. He refused to rejoin the 49ers because of contract differences.

"Raiders general manager Al Davis offered me exactly what I was asking for from the Forty-Niners," recalls Kwalick. "He was paying me fairly. He told me the numbers and I said, 'That's fine.'

"I said to him, there's only one more thing I want, and he said, 'What's that?' I said I want one of those warm jackets for my dad that the players wear, so that when he sits in the end zone on cold days, he won't freeze. So Al picked up the phone and in five minutes the jacket was there. My dad was sitting there. I said, 'Here you go, Dad,' and I signed the contract."

In 1989, Kwalick was inducted into the College Football Hall of Fame. By that time, Kwalick's father had passed away. But his mother and the rest of his family were in State College to share in the ceremonies.

"I felt like I never left the place and I hadn't been there for 20 years," says Kwalick, who today runs a power conditioning firm in California. "You know, when you haven't seen an old friend for a long time, you don't have to go through all the talk. It just feels comfortable."

BOB CAMPBELL

It didn't matter if it was 87 yards or a yard and a half, Bob Campbell's runs usually proved meaningful for Penn State. Take for instance, two runs during the 1968 season: one of them set a record while the other preserved a perfect season.

The 87-yard scoring run against Syracuse helped Penn State beat the Orangemen 30-12 in the final game of the season. The yard-and-a-half run was a two-point conversion that lifted Penn State to a heart-stopping 15-14 victory over Kansas in the Orange Bowl, capping Joe Paterno's first 11-0 season.

Campbell lived for such opportunities in football. He took his big chance in stride.

"That's what you want," Campbell says. "That's where you want to be if you want to play the game."

But before playing for a bowl winner and one of the best teams in Penn State history, Campbell was part of a struggling team in Paterno's first year as head coach. In 1966, Penn State went 5-5 after Paterno took over for Rip Engle. Early in the 1967 season, after a slow start, Paterno shook things up by substituting many of his veterans with a group of talented, young players. The Lions went on to an 8-2-1 season that included a 17-17 tie with Florida State in the Gator Bowl, the first of many bowls for Paterno.

"That was the big change, when all the younger guys started playing," Campbell says. "And I think we just matured to that level. Most of us came from pretty good programs to begin with."

For Campbell, it was a strong high school football program in Vestal, New York, under a coach named Dick Hoover.

"I was very fortunate with the coaches I played for, high school and college," Campbell says. "They were two of the best people I could be around. My high school coach and Joe Paterno were out of the same mold. They were great in how they handled people. And I learned a lot from both of them that I carried on in my own coaching career."

When interviewed in 2004, Campbell was in his fifth year coaching on the football staff at Gettysburg College.

Recalling his Penn State days, Campbell remembers how he hated to practice and how Paterno would get upset with him.

"I loved to play the game," he says. "I loved to do team stuff, but not the practice part of it. Then I became a coach, trying to get kids to do things that I didn't like. It haunted me, because I coached a couple of people like me. They weren't great practice players.

BOB CAMPBELL

Years lettered: 1966, 1967 and 1968
Position: Running back
Accomplishments: Led Penn State in rushing during
the 1966 season with 482 yards and five TDs.

"But it still boils down to when you blow the whistle and the game starts, are they players? If they're players, well, you kind of make your practice around that kind of stuff."

Campbell was a player, no doubt about it. Witness that spectacular 87-yard run.

"It is still the longest scoring run in Penn State history," Campbell says. "There have been longer runs from scrimmage, but they didn't score.

"And what makes that more interesting is that I'm from that area, and I was recruited by Syracuse. And there was a boy who played for Syracuse I played against in high school."

Campbell recalled that the play was pretty simple.

"It was just a quick pitch sweep, toward their bench. It wasn't anything real fancy, just a quick pitch, and off we went."

Campbell says he barely broke a sweat with that run.

"I waited for blockers. It wasn't just an all-out run the whole time. It wasn't one that got me tired out."

It was part of a monster 239-yard rushing day for Campbell, but he's just as well remembered for the mere yard and a half he covered in the Orange Bowl less than a month later. That run capped one of the most exciting finishes in Penn State history. With time running out, the Jayhawks' fans were already starting to celebrate. Their team had a first down on their 38-yard line with only two minutes and four seconds left. Time for the Jayhawks to run out the clock.

However, Penn State had other ideas. Lincoln Lippincott stopped one play for no gain, and Mike Reid threw Kansas quarterback Bobby Douglass for losses totaling 13 yards on two more plays. A good punt by Kansas would have set Penn State back on its heels. But Neal Smith partially blocked the ball, and the Nittany Lions were first and 10 at midfield.

There were 76 seconds left.

"Joe Paterno called [quarterback Chuck] Burkhart and me to the sidelines when we first got the ball back," Campbell recalls.

After getting their instructions from Paterno, Campbell had other ideas as the players headed back on the field.

"That's when I told Burkhart to throw the ball to the left goal post. That's when Joe started yelling at him. We changed the play on the way to the huddle . . . and when we got in the huddle, that's the play that he called."

Only 15 seconds remained.

Burkhart threw the ball exactly where Campbell wanted it. The halfback caught it, and took it down to the three-yard line to complete a daring 47-yard pass play.

"Then the next play, we ran a counter, but Burkhart kept the ball and scored," Campbell said.

It was now 14-13 Kansas. Paterno never liked ties. So instead of kicking the extra point, he instructed his team to go for two.

"Joe called for a pass in the flat to the left," Campbell remembers.

The ball was supposed to go to Campbell, but it was knocked away by the Kansas defense. But a penalty had been called against the Jayhawks because they had too many men on the field. Back into another huddle went the Nittany Lions. One more chance at a two-point conversion.

Bob Campbell is on the football coaching staff at Gettysburg College.
He and his wife Carol have five children.
Photo courtesy of Gettysburg College

The ball was a yard and a half away, moved halfway to the goal line after the penalty was called. Burkhart called the play: Campbell on a run around the left side.

"Personally, through my whole career, if I couldn't make a yard and a half, I don't care who it's against, I don't belong out there," Campbell says. "It was going to go in. I wanted the ball. Burkhart gave it to me."

Campbell didn't remember how big the hole was.

"All I remember was getting in the end zone," he says.

The victory lifted the game, and Campbell, to legendary status at University Park.

After finishing college ball, Campbell played for the Pittsburgh Steelers for one year. By 1970 he was back at Penn State to complete work on his degree. He later added a Masters' while starting on a long and varied career in coaching at both the high school and college level.

He and his second wife, Carol, have five children and two grandchildren. These days the grandkids take up almost as much time as his coaching duties, Campbell says. Maybe when his grandchildren get old enough to understand, Campbell might have a football story or two to tell them about his glory days at Penn State. The thing is, he won't have to exaggerate anything. Just telling the story the way it happened will be quite remarkable by itself.

Where Have You Gone?

DENNIS ONKOTZ

It was 1966 and the Penn State varsity was having problems moving the ball. Not against other teams, against the Nittany Lions' *freshman* team.

"In practice, the first team couldn't run on us," Dennis Onkotz remembers. "They couldn't block me. The handwriting was on the wall."

Indeed. One year later, due to a combination of poor play and injuries to the seniors, Onkotz and a strong group of sophomores took over as starters. After a two-point loss to UCLA, Penn State never lost again until the 1970 season: a school-record 31 unbeaten games in a row. Onkotz and his sophomore buddies had a big hand in the streak.

"I know I was a lot better than the guy ahead of me, it wasn't even close . . . a lot of us were [better than the current starters]." says Okontz, an All-America linebacker at Penn State from 1967-69.

Charlie Pittman led the Lions in rushing as a sophomore, as he would also in his junior and senior years. Joe Paterno's first All-America running back, Pittman would open the doors for such other great backs as Lydell Mitchell and Franco Harris in the late '60s. But, the sophomore-laden defense was perhaps the biggest team star. Along with Onkotz, the sophomore class featured—among others—tackle Steve Smear, safety Neal Smith, linebacker Jim Kates, defensive end John Ebersole and defensive halfback Paul Johnson.

By the time the 1967 season was well underway, 10 sophomores were in the starting lineup. In 1969, when these players were seniors, the Penn State defense set a school record for a 10-game season by holding opponents to 8.7 points a game. In addition, the defense scored 107 of the team's total 312 points with the help of 24 pass interceptions, nine fumble recoveries and three blocked punts. At that point, the Nittany Lions also had future NFL star Jack Ham in the defensive lineup at linebacker.

"I think almost everyone on the defense scored a touchdown," Okontz said.

Onkotz attributed that mostly to Joe Paterno's coaching staff; they had the players in the right places at the right time. Onkotz especially remembers one TD he scored against North Carolina State in 1967.

"Again, it's just great coaching because I knew the play they were running. They tried to isolate Jim Kates, and I just went over to help. I picked it off and picked up a wall of blockers and made a cut and went in for a score. I think that's the one I remember most, because it just was perfect."

Onkotz was also in on the game-saving tackle as Penn State stopped North Carolina State on the one-yard line in the closing minutes. Final: Penn State 13, North Carolina State 8.

DENNIS ONKOTZ

Years lettered: 1967, 1968 and 1969
Position: Linebacker, punt returner
Accomplishments: One of only 12 Penn State players to be named first-team All-America two years in row. Ranks third on the Lions' all-time tackles list with 287. Ranks No. 8 all-time in punt return yardage at Penn State. Inducted into the College Football Hall of Fame in 1995.

The athleticism of the defense fit right in with Joe Paterno's innovative 4-4-3 defensive scheme—four men on the line, four at linebacker and three as defensive backs. Onkotz had been a quarterback and safety in high school before changing positions at Penn State.

"With the 4-4-3, if you have athletic linebackers, the linebackers control the game, as long as you have one or two good defensive tackles," Onkotz says. (Penn State did, with Smear and Mike Reid, who combined for 108 tackles in 1968.) "In that regard, we were able to keep the offense off balance because they didn't know where the rush was coming from."

Many of the players on defense were quarterbacks in high school, so all were quick-footed.

"I was 215 [pounds], Reid was 240, Smear was 230, Ebersole probably wasn't more than 235," Onkotz says. "So we weren't huge, but we were very mobile. We were smart. I mean, that was the thing, we adjusted at the line of scrimmage."

In the years Onkotz and the "Super Sophs" were at Penn State, the Nittany Lions went to three straight bowls. They tied Florida State 17-17 in the Gator Bowl, beat Kansas 15-14 in the Orange Bowl and beat Missouri 10-3 in their second straight trip to the Orange Bowl.

The game against Kansas was decided when the Jayhawks were penalized for having an extra man on the field, giving Penn State another shot at a two-point conversion at the end. The Jayhawks featured future NFL running star John Riggins and mobile quarterback Bobby Douglas. Well, mobile to the extent that Penn State would allow it.

"I don't remember [Douglas] hurting us," Onkotz says. "He tried to run the ball. He wasn't a great passer, he was more of a running quarterback. We had so much speed, he couldn't get outside on us."

Once again, the Penn State defense was well prepared to play against Missouri in the 1970 Orange Bowl. Onkotz had two interceptions in the game, including one that was programmed by linebacker coach Dan Radacovich.

"At halftime, he just drew it up for me: when the quarterback does this, tight end does this, they throw it here . . . and the first time they ran the play I was there and I just got tripped up or I would have gone in for six. But that's the type of coaching we had," recalls Onkotz. "Of course you have to react to it, you have to recognize it, but we were so well coached. The assistants did such a great job with adjustments and things like that."

In 1968, tight end Ted Kwalick joined Onkotz on the All-America team. There is a photo of the two wearing varsity jackets and pointing to a newspaper headline acclaiming their status as Penn State's only All-Americans that season.

"I remember, it was in a letterman's jacket, which I never owned," Onkotz said. "It was a prop. I couldn't afford one."

While the revolutionary movements of the '60s swirled around Penn State and other college campuses, Onkotz said he was too busy to notice.

"I didn't notice it 'til the '70s. I was a biophysics major. I didn't have time to pay attention to anything else. I don't remember watching television in the '60s."

Despite a second straight 11-0 season, Penn State finished a disappointing second in the polls. That was owed to a combination of unlikely circumstances. It was late in the season and the Penn State players voted to go to the Orange Bowl. They didn't know that an upset would spring Texas into the No. 1 spot in the polls. By then it was too late for them to change their minds. The Longhorns, who had been given the presidential seal of approval by Richard Nixon, finished No. 1 after a 21-17 victory over Notre Dame in the Cotton Bowl.

Meanwhile, Penn State's defense was completely shutting down Missouri in the Orange Bowl. Onkotz believes that was the best of the three teams he played on at Penn State.

"We had everyone back in '69, plus adding Franco Harris and Lydell Mitchell as running backs. I thought we were definitely better in '69."

Penn State's unbeaten streak was up to 30 when Onkotz graduated, hoping to make the National Football League. He was drafted by the New York Jets.

"My first year, I broke my leg playing against the Los Angeles Rams," remembers Onkotz. "They put some pins in it. I don't think the technology was as advanced as it is today. But I could not play the following year, I just wasn't physically fit."

Dennis Onkotz, a father of four, lives in the Penn State area with his wife, Diane, and runs a financial consulting business.
Photo courtesy of Dennis Onkotz

During that time, former Penn State assistant coach Dan Radacovich was with the Pittsburgh Steelers.

"He got them to trade for me the year I could not play. The following year I just didn't make it. They cut me, I never got to play again. I just went back to graduate school."

Onkotz eventually settled in the Penn State area and opened a financial consulting business.

"I invest peoples' money, primarily," he says. "I enjoy what I do. I'm my own boss."

He and his wife, Diane, have four children and one grandchild.

With Mount Nittany in full sight and the Penn State campus not far away, Onkotz is constantly reminded of his storied past and the greatness of the teams he played on.

"Everyone knew what they were supposed to do on our teams," he said. "It wasn't anyone trying to be an individual superstar.

"When I played, we thought it was less the talent than it was the teamwork. A lot of the teams we played had great individual talent, but they didn't play as great as a team. A good team can always beat great individuals."

JACK
HAM

J ack Ham has seen it all: An "Immaculate Reception" with the Pittsburgh Steelers, some football miracles at Penn State and a college coach who has been some kind of miracle all by himself. Now Ham, an NFL Hall of Famer with four Super Bowl rings, is back at Penn State as a radio color analyst for Nittany Lions games. He's still amazed by his remarkable journey.

"I played my last game [at Penn State] in 1970, and it is unique in the sense that I come back and do the broadcasting for Penn State football, and it's the same head coach," the former linebacker great says of Joe Paterno's unprecedented reign at University Park.

When Ham took the job on the Nittany Lions radio network in 2000 with play-by-play man Steve Jones, they were replacing Fran Fisher and George Paterno—both institutions at Penn State. Ham certainly wasn't nervous about broadcasting—he had been doing the NFL's *Game of the Week* on Westwood One for some time. But there was a "funny twist" to Ham's taking the Penn State job.

"It was different in a sense that I had to be objective about a guy who was also my presenter at the Hall of Fame," Ham says. "But you have to do it. You have to be fair to the audience as well, so it's something that wasn't a real big problem."

Having Paterno hand Ham a plaque for the NFL Hall of Fame was a lot easier than having Paterno hand him a football scholarship in 1967. In fact, no one was ready to give Ham a full scholarship after he graduated from Bishop McCourt High School in Johnstown, Pennsylvania. A linebacker in high school who also played center and offensive guard, Ham had some interest from Virginia Military Institute. But noting Ham's relatively small 185-pound frame, VMI suggested he first spend a year building himself up at Massanutten Military Academy prep school in Virginia.

"I got knocked around a couple of times and I wasn't getting that many scholarship offers," Ham remembers. "I think East Carolina offered me a partial scholarship. So I thought my football career was over."

Ham thought about going to Penn State as a student and trying to make the football team as a walk-on. Then George Welsh showed up.

"Welsh was the offensive coordinator and quarterback coach at Penn State, and my area was his area to recruit," Ham says. "He asked my teammate from high school, Steve Smear, who was already there for a year, about me."

Smear put in a good word.

"Long story short," Ham says, "I think someone had either turned down a scholarship because they went to Michigan or somewhere else, and I got one of the last scholarships to Penn State [in the 1966 recruiting class].

JACK HAM

Years lettered: 1968, 1969 and 1970
Position: Linebacker
Accomplishments: In 1970, he made 91 tackles and four interceptions and was named to every All-America team. He later was inducted into the Pro Football Hall of Fame.

"Joe always tells the story how stupid the coaches were because I was going to come to college and be a student. I didn't have a whole lot of success in football. And that's why Joe always said, 'We could have had him for nothing, and we ended up giving him a scholarship.' But Steve Smear probably went to bat for me more, and I think they held his opinion in pretty high regard. And that's how I ended up at Penn State."

Freshmen did not play varsity ball in Ham's day.

"You were kind of cannon fodder or scout teams for the varsity," Ham remembers. "But you didn't get involved in competing with the varsity until spring practice of your freshman year."

Ham felt it would be a while before he ever put on a blue jersey, which signified that you were on the first team. He was surprised when he walked into the locker room one day for practice.

"You think as freshmen you start out at the bottom of the ladder, but there was a blue shirt in my locker to start spring practice. And that shocked me. I was on a defensive team with Smear and [Mike] Reid and [John] Ebersole and [Dennis] Onkotz and [Jim] Kates . . . Paul Johnson.

"That's what I remembered most, because all the other freshmen who were going in with me all had second- or third-team jerseys. So I felt it was probably a turning point for me, because I didn't have all that much confidence as a freshman. But Paterno and the coaches had confidence in me, and that's the thing that I remember the most about my inception into the football program."

As a sophomore in 1968, Ham walked right into the middle of a dynasty at Penn State. The Lions went 11-0 in 1968, then 11-0 again in 1969. Not until the second game of the 1970 season, Ham's senior year when Penn State went 7-3, did the Nittany Lions lose during that time. In the interim, the Lions had racked up a school-record 31-game unbeaten streak.

In 1970, Ham was a consensus All-America linebacker. And he says he couldn't have done it without a little help from his friends on the Penn State defensive line.

"With the front four we had . . . Ebersole, Smear, Mike Reid and sometimes Gary Hull, that defense at Penn State was a dominating defense, so I could drop in coverage," Ham recalls. "I could play pass more. That front four set the tone for our defense. There weren't too many teams that could move the football on us. It was fun playing. ...

"And then I got to Pittsburgh and had Joe Greene and Ernie Holmes and L.C. Greenwood. I always appreciated defensive linemen who could make your life a whole lot easier as a linebacker."

The strongest team Ham played on at Penn State? The 1969 team that beat Missouri 10-3 in the Orange Bowl.

"The reason I picked that year was only because of our defense," Ham says. "Missouri had an offense that was averaging about 38 points a game. They had John Staggers, who ended up having a pro career. Mel Gray was a wide receiver and they had just a tremendous offensive team. This offense was a true challenge for us and we held that football team to three points."

Penn State intercepted seven passes, which is still an Orange Bowl record and tied for second highest in any bowl game. Plus, the Nittany Lions recovered two Missouri fumbles.

"For me, I thought our defense was as good as you're going to find in college football," Ham says. "It was just a dominating defense all across the board. You want to play a physical game, we could do that. You want to play a finesse-type game and throw the ball all over the place, we had people who could match up there as well. It was a fun defense to play and, you know, we were always across that line of scrimmage, we were always being aggressive, and doing things. It was hard for college offenses to adjust to our defense."

The Nittany Lions were not only good during their school-record unbeaten streak; they also had some breaks go their way. Against Syracuse in 1969, a penalty gave the Lions a second chance on a two-point conversion after the first one failed. Penn State converted the second time for a 15-14

Jack Ham is a radio color analyst for Penn State games these days and also runs a drug-testing company in Pittsburgh.
Photo courtesy of Jack Ham

victory. It was virtually an exact replica of the year before in the Orange Bowl when Penn State scored on a second-chance conversion for a thrilling 15-14 victory over Kansas. The Jayhawks were penalized for having an extra player on the field.

So Ham was a little jaded with "miracle" finishes by the time he played in the "Immaculate Reception" game for the Steelers on December 23, 1972.

"I got used to games like that. That's why the Immaculate Reception in Pittsburgh when I played was no big deal to me. I already went through with the too-many-men-on-the-field thing in the Orange Bowl."

The Immaculate Reception may still be one of the most controversial pass-catching plays in NFL history. With time running out in their AFC divisional playoff game in Three Rivers Stadium, the Steelers trailed the Oakland Raiders. The ball was on Pittsburgh's 40-yard line with the Steelers facing a fourth and 10. Steelers quarterback Terry Bradshaw threw a desperation pass to receiver Frenchy Fuqua. The ball got to

Fuqua on the Raiders' 35-yard line about the same time as Oakland safety Jack Tatum. The ball squirted into the air, sailing back about seven yards, just as Steelers running back and former Nittany Lion Franco Harris came roaring down the left side. The ball was about to hit the ground when Harris caught it at his shoe tops and raced 42 yards for a touchdown to give the Steelers a 13-7 victory.

Then the controversy started. Under NFL rules, two receivers could not touch the ball in succession on the same play. A defensive player had to touch it between the two to make the catch legal. In reviewing the play, NFL officials ruled that Tatum had indeed touched the ball before Harris caught it. Tatum denied it, swearing only that he had touched Fuqua. But Harris's Immaculate Reception catch stood and gained a life of its own, as did those powerful Steeler teams of the seventies that won four Super Bowls. Ham was one of the stars of the legendary "Steel Curtain" in Pittsburgh.

"That was a great run we had here in Pittsburgh," Ham says. "Just like Penn State, it was a great defense. I was very fortunate to play at both Penn State and at Pittsburgh with solid defenses, so I wasn't getting banged around. Most of my game was speed."

Ham played with the Steelers from 1971-82. Upon retirement from the NFL, he sold coal for a company in the Johnstown area to different power plants, utilities and steel companies.

"I still do some of that, but I also have a drug-testing company as well here in Pittsburgh," Ham says. "We implement drug-free workplace programs for companies, from background checks to drug testing to writing policy for companies, so that's my main job out here."

Ham was sitting in his office in Sewickley, Pennsylvania, when he got a call from Pete Elliott, who was the head of the Hall of Fame at that time. Welcome to the NFL Hall of Fame, Jack.

"I was hoping for it, but still it was a very nervous time for me. Especially when you've been out of the game for five years and you've gone on to do other things in business.

"I thought, you can't do anything about your career at that point. And Joe Greene [of the Steelers] was in the year before me and everybody said they don't like to put too many people [from the same team into the Hall] together. There was apprehension."

Ham's pro credentials were impressive: He was named to the All-Pro team nine straight years and was a unanimous selection on the NFL's Team of the Decade for the 1970s. He was also the NFL Defensive Player of the Year in 1975. He was selected to the NFL Hall of Fame in 1988 and two years later, to the College Football Hall of Fame. Ham thus became the only Penn State player enshrined in both halls.

Nice laurels, but Ham treasures just as much the relationships he made in his football career, especially at Penn State.

"There was still a lot of satisfaction playing with a great bunch of guys," he says.

BOB KNECHTEL

Bob Knechtel knows that offensive linemen are sort of like the engine room of the offense. You don't notice them until something breaks down. Leave it to the football players in the high-profile "skill positions" to set off sparks and get all the credit.

For reference, see the 1971 season, when Knechtel quietly went about doing his job at the right guard position while Lydell Mitchell and Franco Harris were getting all the acclaim. Mitchell was scoring touchdowns like crazy, and Harris was on his way to superstardom in the NFL. However, they couldn't have done it without linemen like Knechtel paving the way.

What was it like blocking for one of the greatest backfield tandems in Penn State history? Lots of fun, Knechtel said.

"The big play at that point in time was a sprint-out draw where they handed off to Lydell and he sort of picked wherever the hole was, and that's where he'd run," remembers Knechtel, now in the financial field in Pennsylvania. "But it was pretty much inside, even though Lydell had a little bit more speed than Franco, and he could get outside. But mostly we were a tackle-to-tackle team."

In 1971, Mitchell led the nation in touchdowns (29) and points (174) and was named to the All-America team before going on to a pro career. Harris did not quite match Mitchell's stats in college, but made up for it in the pros as a Hall of Famer.

"Lydell, of course, had the better [college career]," Knechtel says. "He played tailback in the I formation, so as a result he got a lot more yards rushing than Franco did. But Franco did quite well himself, too."

At the time, the Penn State football program was on the rise in Joe Paterno's early years. For Knechtel, it was a thrill coming out of a steel mill town in western Pennsylvania and going to a major college program that was on the rise. Paterno had replaced Rip Engle in 1965 and it wasn't long before Penn State had become nationally recognized with a 31-game unbeaten streak.

All of this was happening in the midst of Paterno's "Grand Experiment," which emphasized the student athlete.

"Joe was one of the first ones that made kids go to class," Knechtel says. "I lived in a dorm and a fraternity, while other colleges had athletic dorms. This was a new idea."

Knechtel recalls Paterno ruling the football program with a firm hand.

"Joe was a disciplinarian. There was no doubt who was in charge when Joe was around. He was a stickler for details, and I remember more than once, he just had us keep running plays, running plays."

BOB KNECHTEL

Years lettered: 1970 and 1971
Position: Offensive lineman

Knechtel was an offensive tackle at Hempfield High School, near Greensburg, Pennsylvania, a suburb of Pittsburgh. His size was impressive for the time—six-foot-two, 235 pounds. He was recruited by several major schools, and his final choice came down to Penn State or Michigan.

"Penn State was a lot closer to home," Knechtel says. "I felt that my family would have more opportunity to see me play, so I chose Penn State. Back in those days, the idea of picking up and moving 800 miles away just wasn't as common."

In 1968, Knechtel was playing a two-game schedule with the freshman team. He got into his first varsity game as a sophomore in 1969.

"The first game was down at Navy, and I didn't make the traveling team," he says. "There was a bunch of us, and Joe said, 'If you can find your own way down, you can dress for the game.' So my mom and dad and uncle drove me down and I dressed."

Knechtel was pleasantly surprised to get into the game. "It was because we won so easily," Knechtel recalls of that 45-22 blowout.

It was the start of an 11-0 season at Penn State, including a victory in the Orange Bowl. As a sophomore in '69, Knechtel was happy just being part of such a great group of players. He especially loved the red-carpet treatment the Lions received at bowl games.

"They really treated you well, and we stayed at very fancy hotels," Knechtel says. "It was something for a kid coming out of western Pennsylvania and going down there to stay in these hotels with doormen and their fancy uniforms."

Many of Penn State's stars graduated after 1969, and it showed in the results of the 1970 season. Linebacker Jack Ham was the only one to make All-American as the Lions went 7-3 and failed to get a bowl invitation. But even though Penn State did not make a postseason appearance that season, something good was happening at State College.

"We lost three out of the first five games, and then John Hufnagel came in at quarterback and we won the last five games," Knechtel remembers.

The winning continued in 1971. The Lions won their first 10 games, extending their winning streak to 15 and jumping to No. 5 in the national polls. Then they went down to Tennessee and suffered a 31-11 defeat, "We had a couple of key turnovers," Knechtel says. "We were going in for a touchdown, and the quarterback got hit and fumbled the ball, and Tennessee picked it off in mid-air and ran it back for a touchdown. And then they had two kick punt returns for touchdowns. So we got behind the eight ball early and never did recover. It set us back a little bit, so we had one more chance to redeem ourselves."

That would be in the Cotton Bowl, against a powerful Texas team.

The loss to Tennessee did little to help the image of eastern football teams, who seemed to be constantly trying to prove that they were as good as the rest of the country.

"At the time, Texas was quite good," Knechtel says. "This was in the Darrell Royal days and they had just won a couple of national championships. They had just come out with the Wishbone offense."

It was no contest. No contest for Penn State, that is.

Losing 6-3 at the half, the Lions outscored Texas 27-0 after intermission to roll to a convincing 30-6 victory.

Eastern football weak? Ha!

Bob Knechtel, who has two daughters with his wife, Kathleen,
works as a controller for a Pennsylvania business group.
Photo courtsy of Bob Knechtel

"We came out in the second half, early in the third quarter, and Hufnagel hit a long pass," Knechtel says. "And from then on, we started running the ball on them and controlled the second half on the ground.

"To this day, Joe claims that was one of the biggest victories in Penn State's history, because after we lost to Tennessee, everyone was saying well, they're just an eastern team, they're not that good. Then we went down to Texas in the Cotton Bowl and showed them."

After earning a degree in accounting in 1972, Knechtel stayed on at Penn State for a couple of semesters to get education credits for possible work in the teaching field. At the same time, he helped coach the football team.

"I was sort of a graduate assistant coach," he says.

Knechtel then got a job in the financial field in the Pittsburgh area and at the same time earned a master's degree.

"I started out there and have been with the company ever since, in different positions. I've relocated three or four times, but I've basically been with the same company now 32 years. I'm a controller for one of their business groups right now."

In his business life, Knechtel has applied the lessons he learned from playing football at Penn State.

"[I learned from] the experience of playing in a major program, and knowing how much preparation and repetition and discipline you put in to be successful," says Knechtel, who has two daughters with his wife, Kathleen. "Like Joe always said, do the little things right, and the big things will take care of themselves. That has stuck with me."

DAVE JOYNER

All-America football player. All-star wrestler. U.S. Olympic team physician. Dave Joyner, man for all seasons.

Today, Joyner works as a doctor in State College specializing in orthopedics. He had spent a good part of his medical career working as a surgeon. As a college football player, he was doing a different kind of operating.

As an All-America tackle, he was offensive captain of a prolific Penn State team in his senior year. The 1971 Lions scored 484 points, a school record until it was broken 23 years later by the 1994 team. The Lions went 11-1, capping the season with a win over Texas in the Cotton Bowl and a number-five ranking in the national polls.

"That was a great season," Joyner says. "I really enjoyed it. It was my best season, obviously. I got married that year, so everything worked out pretty good."

Playing football for Penn State was a long cherished dream of Joyner's.

"I was very much enthralled [with Penn State]," says Joyner, who grew up in State College. "I started going to football games probably when I was 12 years old, in Beaver Stadium, just after it had been moved. I can remember climbing the fence and sneaking in as a kid. We didn't watch the games so much, because back then the end zones were opened and there was a lot of grass.

"I can remember playing football way out of the way, but during breaks, getting chased around by the cops."

Joyner starred at State College High School, the learning ground for many future Penn State football players. He was part of Joe Paterno's first recruiting class in 1967 that included such players as Jack Ham and Warren Koegel. Joyner was redshirted for a year when he had mononucleosis.

"I practiced the first year without pads because I had mono and I wasn't allowed to hit," he says, "and then my second year was really my true freshman year."

Joyner and Gary Gray were captains of the freshman football team. One of Joyner's early thrills in freshman football was playing at Forbes Field in Pittsburgh, where he dressed in the locker stall of Pirates great Roberto Clemente. Not long after that, the old stadium was dismantled.

"It was raining awful, but that's one of my great memories," Joyner says.

In the spring of 1969, Joyner was finally ready for the varsity. He wasn't sure the varsity was ready for him, however. He was playing behind Tom Jackson, and having "a rough spring."

DAVE JOYNER

Years lettered: 1969, 1970 and 1971
Position: Tackle
Accomplishments: Named to the All-America team in his
senior year. Also, named an All-American in wrestling.
In 1971 Joyner received the first Hall of Fame Scholar-Athlete
award, given to the nation's outstanding scholar-athletes.

"I think Joe [Paterno] saw a lot of potential in me," recalls Joyner, "but I wasn't really producing. I was never lacking in effort, but things weren't quite falling together. I was missing blocks; my timing was off. And maybe part of it was because he was riding me so hard. I mean, Joe was really riding me that spring."

There was a saying around the Penn State football team: When Paterno stopped yelling at you, he didn't love you any more. Joyner felt a lot of "love" that spring.

"He used to come over on the block, and seven-man sled, and I had trouble hitting the sled right. It was such a subtle concept. He wanted you to hit through the man, not to the man, that was the old principle. And evidently, I was hitting to the man on this sled.

"And Joe had this great joy in riding that sled, and blowing his whistle and screaming at the linemen. And every time I'd go, he'd just scream at me because I never got it right."

But Joyner continued to work hard. And by the end of spring practice, he was finally doing things the Paterno way. It earned Joyner a spot in the starting lineup for the 1969 season. Well, sort of. Three into two doesn't usually go. But in this case, it did.

"What ended up happening is we ran three tackles," remembers Joyner. "Jackson and me and Vic Surma would run plays back and forth. So the three of us would play two positions, and that was a big thrill."

Another thrill for Joyner, who also played on special teams: standing next to Paterno on the sidelines.

"That was a great experience for me. I would stand there next to Joe and he'd have his arm around me, and he was getting ready to call plays and he'd talk to himself. He was talking out loud about what he was thinking. You were really intimate, probably closer to the coach than anyone on the football team."

The Lions' most memorable game during the 1969 season had to be against Syracuse. The Lions were losing 14-0 late in the game.

"There were about eight minutes left, and Syracuse had the ball," recalls Joyner. "And I was standing next to Joe waiting . . . because if we changed [tackles], I was ready to run in, you know. And he said, 'They're gonna fumble, they're gonna fumble, they're gonna fumble . . . ' I was thinking to myself, 'He's crazy.' And, sure enough, they fumbled. And we got the ball   . . . against a great defense. I was still thinking, 'Well, wow, gee, it's not over yet.' And we scored."

It was down to about four minutes left, and Syracuse had the ball again.

"And I was standing next to [Paterno] and he was saying, 'They're gonna fumble, they're gonna fumble, they're gonna fumble.' And I was really thinking now, 'The guy's lost it.'"

And sure enough, Syracuse lost the ball again. And Penn State scored to make it 14-13, and the rest is history as the Lions went on to win, 15-14, on a second-chance two-point conversion.

"What I remembered about that [Syracuse] game, and what I learned that season, Penn State football back then had this unbelievable chemistry," Joyner says. "Part of it was Joe, and part of it was the kind of players, and they fed off each other.

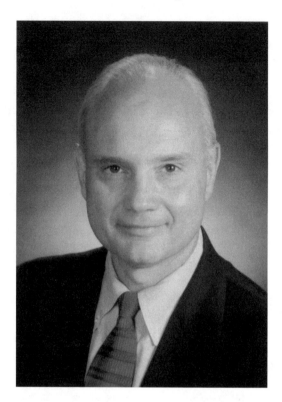

*Dave Joyner is a doctor in State College specializing in
orthopedics and is also involved with the U.S. Olympic
teams and other international medical assignments.*
Photo courtesy of Dave Joyner

"It was just an unbelievable combination of people. And it was more of their emotion
and attitudes than it was their physical capabilities, although they had great physical capabilities."

After losing three of their first five games in 1970, Penn State started another unbeat-
en streak. This one stretched over 15 games into the 1971 season before a loss to
Tennessee in the last game of the regular season.

Joyner, who was one of the Penn State captains that year, remembers it well.

"We beat them in every important statistic, except the one that really counts," Joyner
says of the 31-11 loss at Tennessee. "That was a big letdown. It was a down for me,
because I left from there to go to the Kodak All-American festivities. So I was bound to
some real happy thing supposedly, but I was not feeling that way."

With a 10-1 record, though, Penn State had earned a berth in the Cotton Bowl against
a big and tough Texas team.

"They hadn't failed to score in 80 straight quarters or something," Joyner recalls.

It was a crucial point for the Penn State football program. The loss to Tennessee had
dropped the Lions from No. 5 to No. 10 in the polls and restored the old criticism about

"weak" eastern football. And by halftime in the Cotton Bowl, Penn State had only managed a field goal and trailed Texas 6-3.

"We were running into the locker room and Joe ran up to me on the sidelines," remembers Joyner. "He and I were kind of the last ones off the field. He said, 'How's it going out there? What should I do? What should I say at halftime?'

"And I said, 'Joe, don't say anything. We're just fine.' In other words, I could feel it. I knew what was going to happen. It was like a heavyweight fight, we were pounding them, they were pounding us, but I could tell that they were ready to break."

That's exactly what happened. Penn State scored 27 points in the second half and knocked off a great Texas team to restore some of the eastern football prestige.

"In the third quarter we saw LBJ walking out," Joyner recalls of the Texas-born president, Lyndon Baines Johnson.

Joyner said the loss to Tennessee had served as motivation.

"It brought back all that crap about eastern football, you know. If you think about it, the Big Eight back then was without doubt in my mind the best conference in the country. And we beat the Big Eight champs two years in a row [in the Orange Bowl], and we beat the Southwest Conference champ [Texas, in the Cotton Bowl]."

A team captain and consensus All-American in 1971, Joyner was also a standout wrestler at Penn State. He captained the wrestling team and won the Eastern Intercollegiate Championship three times. In 1971 Joyner was an East-West National All-Star Meet winner and runner-up in the NCAA National Championships. Joyner was also an academic All-American and received numerous awards for his high marks in the classroom.

He soon would make his mark in medicine after graduating from Penn State's Hershey Medical Center. In time, he would found his own Sports Medicine Institute and serve as an orthopedic surgeon at three Pennsylvania hospitals. Somehow Joyner also found time to serve as head physician for the 1992 U.S. Winter Olympic team at Albertville, France, and then chairman of the U.S. Olympic Sports Medicine Committee.

He's still on the Sports Medicine Advisory Committee for the U.S. Olympic Committee. He serves as the administrative hotel physician for the Games, and also as liaison for the on-the-field medical people and the International Olympic Committee. Joyner also serves on the Pan American Games Medical Commission, which governs the medical care and drug testing at the Pan American Games.

As for his own practice, Joyner currently works with a medical group in State College with another legendary Penn State name: Paul Suhey, whose family has had a major impact on Nittany Lion football.

Joyner, a member of the All-Time Nittany Lion Football Team, can claim some extracurricular family involvement in the football program as well. He and his wife, Carolyn, have three sons and a daughter. Two of their sons also played for Paterno, including Matt Joyner, who was on the field for the coach's landmark 300th victory.

Winning, it seems, just comes naturally to the Joyners.

JOHN CAPPELLETTI

When John Cappelletti was going through rookie indoctrination camp with the Los Angeles Rams in 1974, some of the veterans dropped by to check out the celebrated Heisman Trophy winner. One of them, Pat Curran, stopped by his locker and teased him a little about his award.

"Where's your trophy?" Curran asked with a smile. "I want to see your trophy."

"I'm sorry," Cappelletti said, "I don't have it with me."

"I thought you carried it everywhere you went," Curran said.

The two players then broke into laughter. And that was the extent of the razzing that Cappelletti took that season from the Ram vets, or anyone else.

"I don't remember any of the opposing players getting on me about the Heisman," Cappelletti says.

Maybe it was because of Cappelletti's unspectacular playing style: more dash than flash. He was regarded as a solid all-around football player and admired by veterans and rookies alike for his humble, down-to-earth demeanor. Everyone remembered the heartfelt speech he made at the Heisman Trophy ceremony about his younger brother, Joey, stricken with leukemia.

At Penn State, Cappelletti was known for his durability, hard work and coachability.

"I pretty much did what I was supposed to do," he says. "I practiced, I played the games."

In the pros with the Rams, and later the San Diego Chargers, he developed into a fine blocker and pass catcher as well as a strong runner. A tailback in college, the six-foot-one, 220-pound Cappelletti was turned into a fullback in the pros.

"What I did at Penn State was a little more limited probably than what I needed [to do] in the NFL," Cappelletti says. "I really didn't block in college because I was a tailback in the I-Formation, and Bobby Nagle did all the blocking.

"I really didn't catch the ball that much because we were running the ball, and if we were throwing the ball, it was either little screens or something downfield to the wide receivers. But when I went to the next level, I was learning more of the blocking and catching the ball. It came natural to me."

In 1973, Cappelletti was Penn State's "iron horse."

It was "Cappelletti right," "Cappelletti left" and "Cappelletti up the middle" for 286 carries. In one game alone, the running back from Upper Darby, Pennsylvania, carried the ball an astonishing 41 times against North Carolina State.

JOHN CAPPELLETTI

Years lettered: 1971, 1972 and 1973
Position: Tailback
Accomplishments: Penn State's only Heisman Trophy winner. Won the award in 1973 following a season in which he rushed for 1,522 yards and 17 TDs. Posted three straight 200-yard games, then an NCAA record. Also gained All-America honors and later a place in the College Football Hall of Fame.

And the Nittany Lions rode their Iron Horse player to a 12-0 season that included a 16-9 victory over LSU in the Orange Bowl. For his efforts, Cappelletti was rewarded with the Heisman, the only Penn State player to ever win college football's most coveted award.

"It was kind of one of those feelings where the moon and the stars all aligned at the same time and lightning struck," remembers Cappelletti, now a businessman in the pharmaceutical industry in California.

His performance against North Carolina State obviously didn't hurt his Heisman chances. He rushed for 220 yards and scored three touchdowns as the Nittany Lions prevailed in a thriller, 35-29.

"That was a very good game," Cappelletti recalls. "It was probably one of the best games I played in up there, because it was one of those games when it was 7-0, 7-7, 14-7, you know, back and forth all day until the last score, which came late.

"That was probably the best regular season, if not overall, game that I played in. They had a really strong team that year. They came up just looking to knock us off."

Despite the perfect season, though, Penn State only finished fifth in both wire service polls. It was extremely disappointing and puzzling to a lot of people at Penn State.

"What other people did was out of our control," Cappelletti says of the poll voters, "but winning the Heisman probably made up for some of that, as far as it being the first one in Penn State's history. Everybody hopefully got a little satisfaction out of that."

When he first started at Penn State, the notion of carrying the ball a record number of times would never have entered Cappelletti's mind. He was just trying to find a position for himself on a very talented Penn State squad. In three freshmen games, Cappelletti played on both sides of the ball. Then as a sophomore, Cappelletti was made into a defensive back. This was foreign to him—he had been a running back and quarterback in high school.

"I wasn't going to play on offense, because Lydell Mitchell and Franco Harris were still there as seniors. So as a running back, the opportunities were slim and none."

In addition to being on the defensive side of the ball, Cappelletti also did a lot of special-teams work: punt and kickoff returns, holding for kicks, etc.

When Cappelletti's junior season began, Mitchell and Harris were gone. All of a sudden, he was a starting running back.

"Actually, starting the spring of my sophomore year, after the football season, I started making the conversion to running back again," Cappelletti says. "And it was not an easy thing, because the last time I played running back was against other freshmen.

"So now I was playing running back for the first time at the varsity level. It wasn't as easy a transition as I thought it would be. And then once the season started, it didn't come easy for the first couple of games."

Then Cappelletti had a breakout game, and from there he built on his success. Cappelletti wound up rushing for 1,117 yards in his junior year. Not bad, but did it stamp him as a certain Heisman contender heading into his senior year? Cappelletti wasn't so sure.

"Going into that senior year, there were some expectations for the team," Cappelletti remembers. "We had a strong offensive line, and we had a good junior quarterback [Tom

Shuman] who could throw the ball and run the offense. I don't think there were expectations for me as an individual. I don't think anybody was thinking in those terms to a large degree."

Think again. Cappelletti started piling up 100-yard rushing games like they were going out of style. First, a 104-yard day against Navy. He followed that with 187 against Air Force, 151 against Army, 130 against West Virginia, 202 against Maryland, 220 against North Carolina State, 204 against Ohio University and 161 against Pittsburgh. The three games with 200-plus yards was another Penn State record.

By the end of the season, Cappelletti had piled up 1,522 yards and 17 touchdowns. The figures would have been higher had Cappelletti not missed a game against Syracuse with a separated shoulder.

The game against Pitt might have convinced the voters that Cappelletti was a true Heisman candidate. Penn State trailed 13-3 at the half, but rode Cappelletti's second-half ground game to a 35-13 victory. In the process, Cappelletti more than doubled the yardage total of Pitt's Tony Dorsett, another Heisman contender.

After that game, Paterno did some Heisman hyping for Cappelletti.

"He showed his value to this football team," the Penn State coach said. "John Hicks could not have won this football game for us. Cappelletti did."

Hicks, an offensive tackle from Ohio State, was another hot candidate for the Heisman. Along with Cappelletti, there were also several good running backs in the mix: Roosevelt Leaks of Texas; Archie Griffen of Ohio State, Woody Green of Arizona State, Anthony Davis of Southern Cal and Pitt's Dorsett.

When the Heisman voting came in, it was somewhat of a surprise—not because a Penn State player had won it, but because he had won it with such ridiculous ease. Cappelletti's winning margin more than doubled that of Hicks, the runner-up.

At the awards ceremony, Cappelletti gave one of the most memorable and moving acceptance speeches in Heisman history. He dedicated his trophy to his brother, Joey. The story of their relationship was made into a movie, *Something for Joey.*

Cappelletti said it was almost an unreal feeling winning the Heisman.

"I think being from Penn State, that certainly doesn't put you in the limelight all that much," he says. "Back then, Penn State was more of a team concept: you didn't send out press releases on individuals and that kind of stuff.

"So for somebody to win it from Penn State finally, probably that was an oddity in itself. So I think everybody felt like, wow, this is a special deal because it's never happened before."

And it hasn't happened since.

Prior to Cappelletti, Richie Lucas had been the closest Penn State player to winning the Heisman Trophy. In 1959, he finished second to Billy Cannon of LSU.

Cappelletti put the finishing touches on his Heisman season with a touchdown against LSU in the Orange Bowl. That turned out to be Penn State's winning TD, by the way.

"LSU was a very good football team," Cappelletti says. "They were tough, they were quick on defense. They knew what we were going to do. That was probably one of the toughest physical games I had ever been in up to that point."

John Cappelletti lives in California where his business, Alpha Bio, provides goods for bio-tech and pharmaceutical companies. Here he poses in an earlier picture with his wife, Betty, and their sons—Nicholas, John, Thomas and Joseph.
Photo courtesy of John Cappelletti

Nothing compared to the physicality of the pros, of course. In the NFL, Cappelletti earned a reputation as a dependable player. One game against the New York Giants in 1976 was typical of the way Cappelletti could play. In the second quarter, he bolted 10 yards for a touchdown. On the first play of the fourth quarter, he grabbed a seven-yard pass from Rams quarterback James Harris and raced the remaining 25 yards for another TD. Cappelletti's contributions helped the Rams rally from an early 10-0 deficit.

In 1978, Cappelletti led the Rams in ground gaining with 604 yards and added 382 yards in receptions with 41 catches. In 1979, he sat out the season with a groin injury and then was traded to the Chargers. He played four years there before retiring.

"What I learned [at Penn State] certainly prepared me in a lot of ways as far as what it takes to play the game, the fundamentals, learning things the right way."

That would be Paterno's doing, of course.

"There's always a right way and a wrong way to do it, and the least little thing, if it wasn't absolutely correct, he'd notice it and let you know. Joe was tough sometimes, very demanding and a little bit sarcastic.

"There were times I'm sure when a lot of players felt it wasn't right and it wasn't fair. But his job was to make you a better player and create a better team. To do that individually, you had to practice, and you had to practice hard, and you had to practice all the skills. Doing something 90 percent right wasn't acceptable . . . and that's a certain standard that hopefully we've all carried with us throughout the rest of our lives."

After pro football, Cappelletti went into private business in California.

"I've always kind of been somebody that tries to do things on their own first," he says. "I've never really liked to work for anybody."

Cappelletti got into the construction industry, then commercial real estate. Since the nineties, he has been in sales and manufacturing. His company, Alpha Bio, provides goods for bio-tech and pharmaceutical companies.

"We service those industries and the food and beverage industries in California," Cappelletti says. "Central California has a tremendous agricultural base. It's one of the biggest in the country."

Cappelletti has his own special team at home: he and his wife, Betty, have four sons. Naturally, Cappelletti got involved in all of his sons' sports activities.

"Up until about 13 years old, I coached all of them in soccer and baseball and basketball," he says. "I felt I wanted to coach at the youth level, and then once they got to high school, they were kind of going to be on their own.

"I did a lot of youth coaching and enjoyed it. I was able to stay in the area because of the businesses I was in, so I didn't have to travel a lot and I could take on that responsibility of coaching teams."

All in all, a very satisfying life.

"Even though I've had certain postcareer surgical procedures, I feel I'm very fortunate to do all the things that I can do today," Cappelletti says. "I see a lot of guys who played who aren't able to do a lot of things.

"If you were a little bit hurt, or whatever, you still played. You did what it took to get ready for the game. There was a certain peer pressure on you that way."

And, of course, winning a Heisman Trophy must have eased some of that pain.

MARK MARKOVICH

Mark Markovich played his final football game at Penn State on January 1, 1974. The next time he stepped foot on campus was 25 years later. In some ways, coming back to Penn State completed a circle for Markovich. His life journey had a few bumps in the road, but generally was a smooth ride.

"I have nothing but delight that I had opportunities, and don't regret it a bit," Markovich says of his years at Penn State and short but sweet (for the most part) pro football career.

He had a good reason to return to campus—he was the reunion chairman for the 1973 team.

"For the 25th, we had 69 guys back," he says. "And on our 30th, I think there were 69 or 70. It shows the type of group that we had."

And, oh, what a team. The 1973 Nittany Lions had a perfect season at 12-0. They won the Orange Bowl. And they featured the Heisman Trophy winner in John Cappelletti. Markovich was one of the key players on the offensive line that blocked for the great Penn State runner.

"He certainly made all of us linemen look good," Markovich says.

But Cappelletti wasn't the only reason Penn State had so much success that year.

"Tom Shuman had a great year at quarterback," says Markovich, a guard and sometime center who snapped for punts and extra points. "And we had some fine receivers."

Those included Gary Hayman, Chuck Herd, Jimmy Scott and Dan Vatelle.

"There were a lot of weapons there that kept teams off balance," recalls Markovich. "And we had a spectacular defense that got us a lot of turnovers and always had us in good field position."

The defense was anchored by tackle Randy Crowder, linebacker Ed O'Neil and defensive end Mike Hartenstine. It was a veteran team, the type of team that never panicked.

"When there was a tight game, there was calm, there was resolve," Markovich remembers. "You just knew somehow, some way, you were going to find a way to win."

Markovich has always had a special connection with Penn State. He is from Latrobe, Pennsylvania, which also happens to be the hometown of Paterno's wife, Sue. Not only that, but Markovich's mother is a lifelong friend of Sue Paterno's mother.

In his senior year of high school, he had visited seven or eight other colleges before making a trip to Penn State with his parents. After a meeting with Paterno, Markovich was handed over to a freshman host and his parents had dinner with the Penn State coach. In the morning, Markovich met with Paterno again. His meetings with Paterno were unlike any others he had experienced with other coaches.

MARK MARKOVICH

Years lettered: 1971, 1972 and 1973
Position: Offensive lineman
Accomplishments: Academic All-American in 1973.

"I was a tight end in high school," Markovich says. "Joe Paterno was the only one who was honest enough to tell me that I was too slow and didn't have good hands . . . and if I wanted to come to Penn State, I'd be on the line."

Markovich found it a refreshing change from the pampering and gushing he had received from other coaches.

"It was a pretty easy decision," he says. "On my way home, I told my folks that Penn State was where I was going."

Something else that influenced Markovich's decision: Four or five years before, two local athletes had gone to Penn State on football scholarships. One opted to play rugby instead of football in his freshman year. It didn't change the way the Penn State athletic administration treated him. He "was still treated with all the class that you wouldn't expect for someone who had made a change in decision like that," Markovich says.

When Markovich suited up in his sophomore year in 1971, Penn State featured some of the most talented players in school history. He was rubbing shoulders with the likes of running backs Lydell Mitchell and Franco Harris, linebackers Charlie Zapiec, John Skorupan and O'Neil, and offensive tackle Dave Joyner.

When the Nittany Lions lost a game, it was news. It happened at the end of the 1971 regular season, a 31-11 loss to Tennessee after 10 straight victories. There was still a Cotton Bowl game to play against Texas.

"They really shellacked us in the first half," Markovich remembers of the Tennessee game. "In the second we came back, and we really should have won that game."

The seniors, ignited by team leaders Zapiec and Joyner, were determined not to lose again that season.

"Those guys were absolutely beside themselves when we got beat," Markovich says, "and the preparation and the month of practice for Texas, there wasn't any question in anybody's mind what was going to happen in the Cotton Bowl."

Indeed. Final: Penn State 30, Texas 6.

Following that 11-1 season, the Nittany Lions went 10-2 in 1972 before going undefeated in 1973, including a 16-9 victory over LSU in the Orange Bowl. What more could Penn State do to prove its worthiness as college football's national champion? Nothing, as far as Paterno was concerned. So the Penn State coach didn't wait for the results of the wire service polls at the end of the 1973 season. Maybe he knew how they were going to turn out, anyway.

"Joe stood up and declared us national champs," Markovich says. "He bought us beautiful rings."

As it turned out, Paterno's personal poll was far different than the national polls. Penn State finished No. 5 in both the AP and UPI polls despite a 12-0 record.

"Penn State didn't get a whole lot of respect, and there were some other good teams," Markovich says. "But I don't remember anyone whining about it. It was the kind of group that it was more important for Coach Paterno to tell us that we were number one than it was for people that didn't know us to tell us."

The victory capped an extraordinary 33-3 run in Markovich's three varsity seasons.

"It was a very dream-like three-year period," Markovich says. "We'll take the stance that there's never been a Penn State team that had more wins than us over a three-year time period, even though they play more games now."

Mark Markovich runs a machine shop in Peoria, Illinois.
He and his wife, Mary, have three children.
Photo courtesy of Mark Markovich

Markovich was a second-round pick by the San Diego Chargers, one of 10 Penn State players taken in the National Football League draft that year. In addition, several others played pro ball. Markovich and others were also drafted by Philadelphia of the rival World Football League, but opted for the NFL.

At first Markovich almost regretted the decision.

"The start of my rookie year was, I should say, too eventful and memorable for the wrong reasons. It was the year of the strike. San Diego was the first team in camp. We were basically locked into camp, and all the veterans were on a picket line and being held up by the police. It was pretty ugly."

A few days into training camp, Markovich took off for Chicago to play in the college all-star game matching the rookies against an NFL team. But after a few days of practice, the rookies decided they didn't want to play the game until the strike was settled.

"Within hours, our watch guards had whisked us out of our rooms and on a plane back to San Diego," Markovich says. "They called the game off."

Then it was four, five weeks of double-session practices with the rookies and strike-breakers before the strike was finally settled. There was plenty of hard feelings and tension when the veterans came back.

"It was a very tough six-, seven-week period," Markovich recalls.

So was playing with the Chargers once the season got underway. The Chargers were going through a transition period, losing many more games than they won. So when they traded him to Detroit in 1976, Markovich was "very pleased." He earned a starting job with the Lions "and my career was starting to turn in the right direction. I was in the starting lineup on a regular basis," he says.

Then, bad luck struck.

"I suffered really the first injury of my entire career and blew out a knee," says Markovich.

Suddenly, a promising pro career ended, and a private career in business began. Markovich and his wife, Mary, eventually found their way to Iowa Falls, Iowa, a town of about 5,000. They admittedly feel more comfortable in small towns, especially those in the Midwest. In Iowa Falls, Markovich ran a luggage company for 12 years. In 1993, he bought a machine shop in Peoria, Illinois, and moved his family there. The Markoviches have three children, all adopted.

"We've had the wonderful opportunity to adopt three new babies," Markovich says, "and it's just been a real blessing."

As has his relationship with his Penn State teammates.

"We were just a lot of hard-working people that took a lot of pride in what we did, whether it was on a football field or in a classroom," Markovich says.

In most ways, a perfect group.

CHRIS BAHR

When assessing Chris Bahr's kicking game, think long and hard. More precisely, think long and straight. At Penn State from 1973-75, Bahr was known for his booming, breathtaking field goals. It was a sign of the times, he says.

"You have to understand the rules back then," Bahr relates. "When we missed, it went to the 20. So it was like a punt. I think in my senior year, we probably tried 10-14 kicks of 50-yards plus. We probably tried more long field goals than anybody."

Yeah, but what college kids were kicking 55-yarders? Bahr did that three times in the 1975 season, a record that still stands at Penn State. He also kicked three other field goals of 50 or more yards in his college career and holds the Penn State record for 50-yard percentage (six of 15, 40 percent) and field goals attempted in a season (33).

Chris, of course, wasn't the only member of his family to make an impact at Penn State and the sports world in general. Matt Bahr came to University Park a couple of years later and set a few football records of his own. Both went on to successful careers in the NFL, and also played professional soccer with their brother, Casey.

Then there is their father, Walter, a soccer player of international repute who starred on the U.S. National Team and became a successful coach at Temple and Penn State. Not to leave the women in the family out, mother and daughter also made their marks in athletics. Walter's wife, Davies Ann, was a championship swimmer at Temple and his daughter, also named Davies Ann, was an All-America gymnast.

Given the family background, it seemed reasonable that the Bahr boys would boot their field goals soccer-style. And Chris was right in the middle of an evolution when the soccer-style kick was coming into vogue.

"I think people realized it was a more accurate method to kick," he says. "If you would look statistically for kickers prior to soccer style, a guy would lead the National Football League kicking 60 percent of his field goals. Now you kick 60 percent of your field goals through week three, and you're out of work.

"My second year in the league, I was second in percentage with something like 71 percent. I think somebody was at 72. And the league average for the last 15 years has been over 70 percent."

Bahr developed strong legs playing soccer while growing up in Feasterville, Pennsylvania, a suburb of Philadelphia.

"I was friends with the soccer coach's son in high school, and we were kicking in a park and he asked if I wanted to do it in high school," remembers Bahr.

Bahr agreed to give it a try, and wound up playing both soccer and football. He went to Penn State for the same reason.

CHRIS BAHR

Years lettered: 1973, 1974 and 1975
Position: Kicker
Accomplishments: Holds the career record for 50-yard percentage at Penn State (six for 15, 40 percent). Led the Lions with 73 points in 1975. Also played soccer before going on to a successful pro football career.

"I wanted to go to the school where I could kick and play soccer at the same time," he says. "Penn State offered that opportunity, and it cost less than other schools."

Between football and soccer and his studies, Bahr was a busy young man.

"I used to fly to [football] games by myself at times, because we played Friday night soccer, and I'd have to hop on a plane or drive wherever they were playing."

At times it got complicated. Football coach Joe Paterno wasn't always happy to share Bahr with the soccer team.

"Paterno wasn't too pleased when I showed up for a game with Iowa. I'd flown out," remembers Bahr. "I'd taken a shot to the side, and I could barely walk."

"He wasn't thrilled that I wasn't able to kick when I got out there. So he actually put me on the sidelines for a few weeks. But it was always something that could have happened. I had said from the beginning, if they made me choose a sport, I was going to play soccer. So, fortunately, they didn't make me choose."

A story about Bahr that few people know:

"I almost transferred to Temple after my second year in school. I knew my first two years I wasn't going to kick. They had this Al Vitiello. And I had looked at the schedules for soccer and football for that next year, and there were four days that there was a soccer game and a football game at the same time. And so I figured that wasn't going to work."

Bahr talked to his father, then the Temple soccer coach, and football coach Wayne Hardin. They had no problem with Chris playing both sports.

"So I was going to transfer to Temple," Bahr says. "And one thing led to another. I went up to Penn State for a meeting just to explain it to them, and when I got to the meeting, there was only one conflict left on the schedule, so I stayed. My one conflict, I went and played soccer."

Chris would eventually play soccer for his father at Penn State after Walter Bahr moved to State College in 1974.

It was Bahr's long kicks in football, however, that put him in the national spotlight. One of his biggest: a 44-yarder in the 1974 Orange Bowl that helped Penn State beat LSU 16-9 and complete the first 12-0 season in school history.

"I don't remember much about it, other than I hit it good," Bahr says.

When the final polls came out, Penn State was ranked number five in the country despite a perfect record.

"I think we deserved the national championship as much as anybody," Bahr says. "I don't think people realized how good that team actually was, because we played what was perceived as a softer schedule. You had a lot of talent there. I mean, for 20 of those guys to play professional football afterwards, you had to have some talent."

In 1975, Bahr made 18 of 33 field goal attempts and led the Nittany Lions with 73 points in a 9-3 season. Although the pressures of winning were sometimes squarely on Bahr's shoulders, he enjoyed the challenge of coming in to kick in crucial situations.

"I sort of channeled nervous energy into positive energy. I was always nervous," says Bahr. "… Professionally I was always better in bigger games, because I concentrated more, I guess. I was fortunate to be on two Super Bowl teams that won."

That would be the Raiders, who were then in Los Angeles.

Chris Bahr lives with his family in State College, where he is in the financial services business and also coaches children's soccer teams.
Photo courtesy of Chris Bahr

In Super Bowl XV, Bahr kicked two field goals, including one for 46 yards, and three extra points, as the Raiders beat Philadelphia 27-10. In Super Bowl XVIII, he kicked a field goal and five extra points as the Raiders knocked off Washington, 38-9. Bahr spent the majority of his 14-year NFL career with the Raiders.

After retiring from pro football, Bahr worked as a lawyer for a couple of years before going into the financial services business. He eventually came back to State College to live and work for the Provest Management Group, a Columbus, Ohio-based firm that handles investments for athletes.

Bahr, married with two sons, also coaches children's soccer teams and helps Penn State soccer on a volunteer basis.

Just like his years at Penn State, Bahr hasn't found too much time to sit still.

Where Have You Gone?

MATT BAHR

It's up—it's good!

That's what you usually heard from the announcer whenever Matt Bahr was kicking the ball—whether it was a field goal or an extra point. He was not the first in the Bahr family to kick for Penn State, of course. Older brother Chris had played for the Nittany Lions from 1973-75 and set an NCAA percentage record for kickers.

Then Matt came to University Park a couple of years later and broke his brother's record in 1978. He connected on 22 of 27 field goals for an 81.5 percentage. But, Matt didn't keep tabs.

"I never kept track of that . . . I really didn't," Matt says. "Like Joe Paterno said, the bottom line is to win. Did you help your team? Were you a part of the effort?"

As Bahr recalls, Paterno told his players: "Do as well as you can and good things will happen."

Good things usually did to Penn State when Bahr was in the lineup. The 1978 season was statistically his best. Four times, Bahr kicked four field goals in a game, and he was a perfect 31 for 31 on extra-point kicks. Along with quarterback Chuck Fusina, he was a key part of Penn State's high-powered offense. The Nittany Lions outscored opponents 326-97 and went undefeated that season before losing by one touchdown to Alabama in the national championship game.

"I had some great teammates, we came up a little short in the end," Bahr says. "But that's why they play the game, that's the fun part."

That was the year that Fusina finished runner-up in the Heisman Trophy voting.

"Chuck got us there," Bahr says. "In my estimation, there's no one I would have rather played with at that position. He always got it down to where we had a chance to score a touchdown, or settle for a field goal."

Bahr's excellent college career was only a warm-up, as it turned out. He went on to a remarkable 18-year career in the NFL, winning two Super Bowl rings.

That success on the gridiron was a far cry from his roots, which like his brother, Chris, and father, Walter, lie in soccer. With his ability to kick a soccer ball at his high school in the Philadelphia area, kicking a football came quite naturally to Bahr. But kicking at Penn State was not in his plans.

"I was originally going to the Naval Academy," he says. "I was going up to there to play soccer and play football, too, for George Welsh.

"But the Naval Academy was changing the soccer coach and that would seem to be too much of a chance to take. Penn State had recruited me, too. So I accepted the offer at Penn State."

MATT BAHR

Years lettered: 1976, 1977 and 1978
Position: Kicker
Accomplishments: Remembered for his kicking accuracy on the gridiron in both college and the pros. In 1978 at Penn State, he didn't miss in 31 extra-point attempts. Also made 22 of 27 field goals for an 81.5 percentage to break the accuracy mark of his brother, Chris. Played both football and soccer.

At the time, Chris was playing both football and soccer. He wasn't the only one whom Matt knew at Penn State. His father, Walter, happened to be the Penn State soccer coach. Walter Bahr told the Penn State student newspaper that he showed no favoritism toward either of his sons. In both cases, it worked out fine.

It was as a football player, however, that Chris and Matt became nationally renowned. Like the postal service, the Bahrs delivered in rain, snow and sleet. Witness Matt's performance against Pitt on the last day of the 1977 regular season.

The wintry conditions were treacherous. The teams were slipping and sliding all over the Astroturf at Pitt Stadium.

"The light snow that fell throughout the game gave the defenses the advantage as the footing became so poor that runners and receivers could not cut the way they wanted," wrote Gordon S. White, Jr., in *The New York Times.*

But at least one player had the footing he wanted. That was Matt Bahr, who connected on field goals from 34, 31 and 20 yards. The last field goal provided the winning margin as Penn State put on a goal-line stand to survive, 15-13. Many agreed it was one of the most thrilling games between the two longtime rivals.

"From a personal perspective, the one game that sticks out in my mind, only because I was successful in what I felt were very unfavorable conditions, was the Pitt game," Bahr says. "The field as I recall was very icy."

That victory earned Penn State a trip to the Fiesta Bowl. There, Bahr kicked two field goals and four extra points as the Nittany Lions beat Arizona State, 42-30.

"That was a gun fight," Bahr recalls. "It was back and forth, a very exciting game."

Bahr kicked other important field goals in his Penn State career—39 in all. That number is not the thing he remembers most about his years at Penn State, though.

"The players lived in the general population, the student population," says Bahr, who was enrolled in the electrical engineering program. "And so the college experience was, you got it all. You were part of student life, and that's the way Joe Paterno wanted it. That's the way it should be."

There was another reason that Bahr appreciated going to Penn State: the coaching. He said he owed a good deal of his success to the preparation he got from Paterno.

"Joe is amazing. He could be 300 yards away on the practice field, you make a mistake and you hear about it. And you can hear that voice railing at you from across the way, so you knew his eyes are always on you."

When Bahr graduated from Penn State, he went from one good team to another. This time, he was a kicker for the Super Bowl-champion Pittsburgh Steelers. As a rookie, he kicked a 41-yard field goal to help the Steelers win their fourth straight NFL title.

Remembering lessons learned at Penn State, Bahr also took classes. He eventually earned a master's degree in business.

"I went to school in the offseason," he says. "Again, that was part of the advice given at Penn State with careers being so short in the NFL. You'd be foolish not to try to prepare for postcareer, because football was going to be brief at best."

Normally, yes. In Bahr's case, he managed to stick around the NFL for nearly two full decades—about 14 years longer than the average. Along with Pittsburgh, Bahr also played for San Francisco, Cleveland, the New York Giants, Philadelphia and New England. He won his second Super Bowl ring with the Giants in 1991.

That was the season that Bahr literally kicked the Giants into Super Bowl XXV. In the NFC final, he booted five field goals, including a 42-yarder with time running out, to give New York a 15-13 victory over San Francisco. Then the Giants upset Buffalo 20-19 for the NFL championship. Guess who booted the winning field goal for the Giants? That's right, Bahr, on a 21-yarder with 7:20 to go.

"We were severe underdogs against the Bills, but that goes back to the Penn State experience. We were underdogs, but that didn't mean that we didn't feel we had a good chance of winning. And we did."

Facing such pressure situations didn't seem to faze Bahr. Throughout his college and pro career, he was uncommonly cool in such circumstances.

"That was a part of the job," he says, "the good part. The worst that could happen, you miss, you go home. No one died."

In his 18 years in the NFL, Bahr connected on more than 73 per cent of his field goals. Another remarkable stat: In 482 attempts, he only missed 10 extra-point kicks.

His accuracy of success in the business world is just as efficient. Since retiring from pro football, Bahr has kept busy in a variety of endeavors. He first put his electrical engineering degree to good use at Westinghouse. He later opened an internet-based business designing custom uniforms for sports teams. Bahr also got involved in a fitness program to educate America's school kids about the national problem of obesity. The program tries to encourage a more active lifestyle for school-age kids, getting them away from TV and computer games and out into the fresh air.

"I've got a lot on my plate," says Bahr, who has two daughters and a son with his wife, Maresa.

And a well-balanced life.

"That's what I always try to tell kids: If you can go on to the next level with the NFL, that's fine. But get a good education while you're in school and make the most of your experience. And I think I did both."

PAUL SUHEY

At Penn State, it's usually a family feeling among the football players. One particular family can say that literally.

"This will be the fourth generation—I don't think that's going on anywhere else in the country," says Paul Suhey, a member of Penn State football's "First Family."

That's not exaggerating. The generational lines in Suhey's family go back to Bob Higgins, who played at Penn State from 1914-17 and again in 1919 and coached the Nittany Lions from 1930-48. Higgins was only one of five football players in Penn State history to letter five years. Steve Suhey, an All-America lineman in the 1940s, married Higgins's daughter, Ginger. They had seven children—and three of them played football at Penn State: Larry, Paul and Matt.

And in 2004, Paul's son, Kevin, was on a football scholarship preparing to start classes at Penn State.

"He had the chance to go other places, and he didn't want to," Paul Suhey says of his son, who played quarterback at State College High School, another family tradition. "He wanted to go to Penn State. We weren't going to argue with him. We thought that was a pretty good decision, too."

As it had been for other generations of Suheys. Steve Suhey not only married Higgins's daughter, he played for the coach they called "The Hig."

Suhey, a 210-pound guard, was a key part of the 1947 Penn State team that went undefeated and set national defensive records that still stand. He had played in 1942, went away to war, and returned for the 1946 and 1947 seasons. Suhey, fast and agile, led the ball carrier on most plays. Line coach Joe Bedenk said he was the best guard he ever coached.

"The funny thing with Dad," says Suhey, "he didn't talk much about the Second World War, and he didn't talk much about football.

"I mean, football was a big part of our life. We enjoyed the Penn State games and we understood that my dad played there. But he didn't really brag about it, that he was an All-American. He really didn't say he played with the Pittsburgh Steelers a little bit. He just basically allowed us to enjoy Penn State football at that time."

Paul Suhey, now a physician/surgeon in State College, remembered going to games to sell programs and "a lot of people" coming over to the house after the game.

As for his famous grandfather, Suhey said: "We were around him enough as kids, but we didn't quite understand him as a football coach, or an ex-football coach at that time. Unfortunately he had a stroke and was paralyzed on one side, but he was still real fun, and he loved to get around and play checkers."

PAUL SUHEY

Years lettered: 1975, 1976, 1977 and 1978
Position: Linebacker
Accomplishments: In senior year, won the Ridge Riley Award
for "sportsmanship, scholarship, leadership and friendship."

One of Suhey's fondest recollections of his grandfather involved a prized football that had some historic significance to Higgins.

"My grandfather had an autographed football painted with the score. I forget [which game], Army or something, and all signed. And we took it out and played with it," recalls Suhey. "We didn't pay much attention to all the stuff on it. To us, it was just another football. We had a catch with it. We had a great time, we actually scuffed it up pretty good."

But Higgins didn't care.

"He thought it was funny. My mom actually didn't get too upset with us, either. It was a great ball. To have that kind of a ball at that age, a real, true leather ball was nice. We always laughed about it."

Higgins, a legend at Penn State for so many years, died when Paul Suhey was in the sixth grade. That was 1969.

At that time, Paul and his brothers were becoming steeped in the Penn State tradition while growing up in State College.

"As a kid growing up in this town you were always listening to the radio on Saturday, or either playing while you were listening … trying to mimic what was going on. So we were always rolling around in the grass and playing with a football," remembers Suhey.

There were four brothers and three sisters, and they all participated in some kind of sport.

"We did anything that was involved with sport. Whether we were playing baseball, soccer, football, basketball, wrestling, we did anything that was available at the time. We had all kinds of equipment around the house with seven kids.

"Back then you didn't have TV, computers, you didn't have things that kids have nowadays. You had to get us out of the house, you had to do something. Fortunately we lived right behind the high school, so our back yard opened up to the practice field for the soccer team. So we'd just go out and do something."

Suhey said his father didn't put any pressure on the kids to play football, to try to follow in his footsteps. But they just fell into the sport at local State College High School, one of the top schoolboy programs in Pennsylvania.

"We were lucky," Suhey says. "We had a good coaching staff, a good head coach, Jim Williams. We lost one game in four years. We won 36 games in a row. It was fun."

Larry Suhey, a fullback, was the oldest of the three football-playing brothers. He went to Penn State first. It was assumed that Paul, next in line, would follow. Even with his Penn State blueblood inbreeding, Paul wasn't so sure.

"I was sort of in between," he recalls. "I thought maybe it would be good for me to go away. I had some interest in medicine. I looked around a good bit, at least on the East Coast."

Then he had a talk with Larry and changed his mind.

"I was thinking why should I go eight hours away when I can get the same thing two miles away, in my own back yard? Larry made me realize that."

Then the two of them worked on Matt, a running back who had all kinds of offers from around the country.

"I think Matt was also thinking maybe he was going to go [someplace else], but we grabbed him and said, 'Hey, no, no, no!' We sort of got a little sentimental with him and

Paul Suhey, an orthopedic surgeon, has a medical practice in State College, where he lives with his wife, Carolyn. They have four children.
Photo courtesy of Paul Suhey

said, 'We're here, you come here. We're all in the same bag. You know, we can keep an eye on you. Why go away?'

"Down deep, I think it probably made my parents happy that we all decided to come here, but they didn't pressure us."

Because Larry had torn up a knee, he was red-shirted. That gave him an extra year of eligibility and allowed the three brothers to play together for one season in 1976.

"It was nice," Paul Suhey remembers. "It was comfortable. I could help Matt and Larry could help me. Actually, we were around the [football players] a lot, and knew the other guys. So there was no question it was an easier transition [than going to another school], especially being local to begin with."

Larry was the starting fullback until hurting his other knee. While he was out, Matt was switched from tailback to fullback. Paul was a linebacker.

That 1976 season wasn't only a growing process for the Suhey brothers, but for the entire Penn State team. The Nittany Lions had a lackluster 7-5 record, losing to Notre Dame in the Gator Bowl.

The 1977 season was different. Penn State went 11-1, losing only to Kentucky by four points. The Lions then reeled off eight victories, finishing with a 42-30 decision over Arizona State in the Fiesta Bowl.

"After the loss to Kentucky, I think we were coming into our own," Suhey says. "We were just getting back to where we needed to be. And then in '78, we had the confidence coming out of the '77 season. We knew we had some good kids coming back."

They included quarterback Chuck Fusina, tackles Bruce Clark, Matt Millen and Keith Dorney, safety Pete Harris, kicker Matt Bahr, linebacker Lance Mehl and receiver Scott Fitzkee. And, of course, Paul and Matt Suhey.

"First game, we weren't that dominant [a 10-7 victory over Temple]," Suhey remembers. "Then we got on a roll."

The Nittany Lions won their next 10, including a revenge beating of Kentucky. It was a game that Paul Suhey vividly remembered.

"We had lost to Kentucky two years in a row," Suhey says, "so I thought that was a jinx.

"In my senior year we went down there to play them. I distinctly remember some of the games we lost to those guys. Usually we played one o'clock games in those days. We actually played a Saturday night game and put a pretty good thumping on those guys."

Penn State cruised, 30-0.

"That was just a good game. It allowed us to put those guys behind us. We played in beautiful Kentucky Stadium in the evening. It was just a great atmosphere. We were confident that we needed to show these guys that they just couldn't come up and beat us any old time."

After an 11-0 regular season, the Lions were ranked No. 1 in the country. They faced No. 2 Alabama in the Sugar Bowl for the national championship. It ended in a 14-7 loss and a bitter disappointment for Penn State.

"We knew we were better than them," Suhey says. "They knew we were better than them. We just lost that day. We just did not play well."

After graduation, Suhey tried out for the Dallas Cowboys as a free agent, but was cut. He then went to medical school. For a while he was involved with the Alabama Sports Medicine Institute in Birmingham, Alabama.

In 1990 he established a private practice in orthopedic surgery in Jacksonville, Florida. After seven years he moved back to State College and set up his practice there.

"I just missed family and got tired of the hot weather," he says. "[Florida] was great when the kids were younger."

But the Suheys preferred a simpler life and preferred to be closer to their roots.

"Here you've got one high school and one hospital and sort of a one- community feeling. I just thought that was a better place to raise kids," says Suhey, who has four children with his wife, Carolyn.

And of course, there are the long-standing ties that Suhey has with Penn State football.

TONY
GORDON

There's Eastern Standard Time. Daylight Savings Time. And then there's Joe Paterno Time.

Joe Paterno Time?

"I'm going to be 49," Tony Gordon says, "and my watch is still 15 minutes fast—Paterno Time."

Setting your watch ahead to make appointments on time wasn't the only lesson the one-time safety learned from Paterno, who was part-time father figure and full-time perfectionist.

"Push yourself . . . work hard to attain your goals . . . have integrity," Gordon says. "There are a lot of things I learned from the Penn State program."

Gordon, who played in the '70s, says he "would hang on a cross" for Paterno. That is, now after seeing how much of an impact the Penn State experience has had on his life. As a star high school athlete, however, he was less than enthusiastic about becoming a Nittany Lion. Growing up in Cleveland, Ohio, Gordon was enamored of the Big Ten. An all-stater in football, basketball and baseball, he was recruited by Ohio State, Michigan and Notre Dame.

"Everybody knew about Joe Paterno, and what a great and well-respected program he had," says Gordon, who played tailback and strong safety in high school. "But I wanted to go to Michigan. I liked the 105,000-seat stadium."

He did visit Penn State, but only as a concession to his parents.

"Joe invites your parents and encourages them to come," Gordon says. "My dad couldn't make it that weekend. At that point, he was running a gas station. But my mom went up."

Gordon spent a few days going around with some of the Penn State players. Gordon's mom, meanwhile, spent time with Paterno.

"I didn't see my mom for a while, and all of a sudden, she just made it very clear: 'You're going to Penn State!'"

Gordon was unhappy, "to the extent that I ran away from home. I just went down the street and stayed at my buddy's house. I wanted to go to Michigan.

"I'll never forget what my mother said. She said Joe told her: 'Mrs. Gordon, I don't know if he's going to play or not, but I know he'll graduate with an education. We'll always take care of him.'"

At Penn State, Paterno tried to find a place for Gordon. One of the positions he tried was linebacker. Penn State was known as "Linebacker U" for all the great players the Nittany Lions had turned out at that position.

TONY GORDON

Years lettered: 1977
Position: Played a variety of positions, including safety

"He doesn't care if you're an All-America quarterback, he's going to try you at linebacker," Gordon says of Paterno. "So at some point in time, in everybody's career at Penn State, you were tried at linebacker."

Gordon ended up playing a variety of positions on the Penn State varsity, including safety.

"I was on kickoff and specialty teams," he says. "But . . . at that point of time, you played and did whatever you could to win."

Gordon was part of one of Penn State's best teams—the 1977 squad that went 11-1, losing only one game by four points. Truth is, not much was expected of the Lions following a 7-5 season in 1976.

"After we had spring practice," Gordon says, "we had a meeting before we left to go home. We said, everybody thinks we're going to be terrible, but we're going to work hard, and we're going to win."

Paterno was especially strict about his players' appearance, on and off the field.

"We couldn't wear T-shirts to class, we had to wear collared shirts, tucked in, and we had to wear socks," Gordon recalls.

"You could have your hair long, but the white guys' hair couldn't be more than an inch below the ear. Joe would measure it. If it was longer, he would cut it. With the black guys, you'd get the ruler, it was like checking the oil. He dipped it in, if it was above a certain height, time for a haircut. I'm not kidding—I got many Paterno haircuts, Paterno and Suhey haircuts. Larry, Matt and Paul all cut hair real good."

Paterno was making his impact felt long after the kids left school. Said Gordon:

"I tell people this and they laugh. I was at a cocktail party last year, with some former players. We were at the bar having a few cocktails. All of a sudden, here comes Joe. We were all trying to hide our drinks."

The Nittany Lions opened the 1977 season with a 45-7 pounding of Rutgers, then beat a strong Houston team, 31-14. The Cougars were ranked No. 9 in the country. Then came another important test for Penn State: the Maryland game.

"Maryland was 3-0," Gordon says. "They were always tough. We played against the Ohio States and the Notre Dames . . . we played against Alabama. Maryland was always tougher. So we knew it was a big game. I think of any game, it told us where we were as a team if we went out and beat them.

"We were a little nervous in the locker room."

Just before the Lions took the field, the usually reserved John Dunn got up and said quietly, "Adversity is the true test of greatness."

"The whole locker room went crazy and we ran out on the field and we blew them out," Gordon remembers.

Final: Penn State 27, Maryland 9.

"I think it was the defining moment for that season," Gordon says. "We kind of knew that we were pretty good."

Even after a 24-20 loss to Kentucky the following week.

"We wanted to finish the rest of the season strong and hope to get a shot at a major bowl."

Adversity is the true test of greatness. The Lions remembered Dunn's quiet eloquence of the week before and just went back to work. Utah State, Syracuse, West Virginia,

*Tony Gordon lives in Jersey City, New Jersey, and does logistics
work in the field of international freight forwarding.*
Photo courtesy of Tony Gordon

Miami, North Carolina State, Temple and Pitt fell to the Lions. They finished the season with a 10-1 record and earned a berth in the Fiesta Bowl vs. Arizona State.

There Gordon remembers that the Nittany Lions received some extra motivation unwittingly supplied by Arizona State wide receiver John Jefferson.

"Arizona State under Frank Kush was always known as a passing school, finesse, graceful," Gordon says. "I guess John Jefferson was asked to compare the Penn State team to Arizona State. He said, 'It's like a bunch of thoroughbreds going against a plow horse.' You know, us with the big, black shoes and dull uniforms and Arizona State with patches all over their helmets, quick, flashy, and all that. So that set us off."

An inspired Penn State team went out and whipped Arizona State 42-30, handing the Sun Devils their first bowl loss in six postseason games. The Nittany Lions wound up ranked No. 4 in the country in the UPI poll and No. 5 with AP.

And Gordon moved on, first working with the highly respected international transportation company called the Flying Tigers. He was hired by former Penn State player Chuck Franzetta, who was regional manager for the company. Gordon later followed Franzetta to New York when Chuck got a director's job with *Newsweek*. Fast forward to 2005 after a couple of career changes and Gordon is back doing what he likes best: logistics work in freight forwarding.

He has good and bad days, but always keeps applying the lessons he learned at Penn State.

"That's the resilience, you keep coming back," says Gordon, who is married with a daughter. "When you get knocked down, you feel yourself going down, you think about getting back up. It's a Paterno thing . . . preparation, always be prepared."

MIKE MUNCHAK

Mike Munchak was all set to leave the house for his daughter's basketball game. But first he thought he'd take a peek at the TV. The National Football League Hall of Fame was to make its announcement of new selections that morning—naming the "Class of 2001." Munchak was one of the 15 finalists.

"I wasn't really getting excited about it," he says. "For a lineman, it's kind of hard [to get elected]. Unless you have a no-brainer, you play 20 years, or 18 years. I was glad I was being mentioned. To make the final 15 was a thrill in itself for me."

Finally, a sportscaster announced that seven players had been chosen for the Hall.

"I thought, that's pretty good, seven out of 15, that's the max you could have in any one year," Munchak says. "So he starts rattling off the list. Randomly he was giving names out."

Suddenly, "time stopped" for Munchak.

"He said, 'Mike,' and I knew I was the only Mike ... and he said 'Munchak.' I thought, Did he really say that? There's no way he said that.'"

As soon as he did, the phone starting ringing.

"I knew my family and other people were watching the show. It was a pretty exciting time, and I was just like in shock."

The former Penn State player had made the Hall—one of only five Nittany Lions in history so honored. And Munchak doesn't think it could have happened without the Penn State experience. The all-pro guard believes that with unflinching certainty.

"Obviously Penn State was a huge, huge part of that," he says of his selection to the Hall of Fame. "If I went somewhere else, it may not have happened to me."

He almost did go somewhere else. Munchak, a Pennsylvania high school product, wasn't sure he would fit in as a player at Penn State.

"I think my biggest problem was that I didn't know what position I'd play," he says. "And I think no one else really knew, either."

Munchak was a fullback and linebacker in high school, but was told he didn't have the speed for those positions in college.

Offensive line? No, not there, either.

"I wasn't really a lineman, I wasn't built like a lineman," Munchak says. "I was 6-3, 240."

Plus, he felt he would have a hard time cracking the Penn State team, which usually consisted of the top recruits in the country.

"I thought for a while I was going to go to Syracuse or Maryland," he recalls.

And then Joe Paterno visited his house one day and changed his mind.

MIKE MUNCHAK

Years lettered: 1979 and 1981
Position: Offensive lineman
Accomplishments: Enjoyed a Hall of Fame career
in the pros with the Houston Oilers. Selected
for the Pro Bowl nine times in his NFL career.

"That really influenced me a lot," Munchak says. "He took the time to come to my house when he thought I would go somewhere else. I didn't really see myself as a top-level recruit at the time.

"I thought if I make it there at Penn State, as far as football goes, great! And if I don't, I know that Coach Paterno wasn't going to let me get lazy with schoolwork. That was very important to him."

Munchak felt good about his decision—until he arrived at Penn State.

"I thought, 'What was I thinking about?' I saw the type of guys they did have there, and I knew it was going to be one heck of a challenge."

Paterno and his staff weren't sure at first where Munchak should play.

"When you come in to the meeting room the first day, there are about 100 players there," recalls Munchak. "And they say, 'Okay, offense on one side and defense on the other side,' and they're passing out the playbooks.

"I was sitting on the defensive side, figuring I was going to be a linebacker of some sort, or a defensive end. I was waiting as they were passing out the books and I didn't have a book. All of a sudden, they yelled out my name, and said, 'Hey, you're on this side. You're playing offense!'"

Munchak was surprised.

"I knew I was not playing running back. And they moved me to tight end, and I thought, 'You've got to be kidding me.' And they didn't have a book for me. And they gave me some stuff to study. So I'm studying tight end routes, and I ran them for one day in practice. We were out there for about 10 minutes and ran a few different things, and the next day I came into practice and I had a note to go see Coach Paterno."

Paterno told Munchak to turn in his book, he was going to play on the defensive line.

"I said, 'What happened to tight end?' He goes, 'Are you kidding me, I saw you run two routes—you can't play tight end.'"

So Munchak played "D-line" with such stars as Matt Millen and Bruce Clark.

"And I was thinking, 'What am I doing here? Those are two Parade All-Americans.'"

That lasted about a week. Then several players on the offensive line got hurt. Guess where Munchak's next stop was?

"They called me in and Joe moved me over to the offensive line. They needed help running the 'show teams' to get the varsity ready for the season."

Munchak played offensive tackle, which he had never played before. He was beginning to stretch as a football player in more ways than one.

"What helped me most that whole year was going against Bruce Clark and Matt Millen in practice, because I was giving them the look of the team they were going to play," Munchak says. "So I went against great, great players in practice every day, like linebackers Lance Mehl, and [Paul] Suhey. I saw some of the best in the country in practice, and they made me compete because they wanted good looks. I think that really helped me develop as a lineman."

Munchak also improved physically with the help of strength coach Dan Riley and technically with the help of line coach Dick Anderson.

"By spring ball, I had gained about 20 pounds. That kind of got me in the competition of playing offensive line at that time," Munchak says.

Munchak also gives tremendous credit to Anderson for his development as an offensive lineman.

"He taught me how to play the position. He was very much into technique, and very meticulous. He was always on top of you, not cutting you any slack, making sure you were doing it right. Footwork, head placement, everything was exact, and he was a stickler for it."

As a freshman, Munchak saw limited action, mostly on special teams. One of his first early thrills: he was put on the traveling squad for the national championship game against Alabama in the 1979 Sugar Bowl.

"That was awesome, to be a part of that. I was just excited that year that I wasn't red-shirted, and that I was able to travel with the team."

In his sophomore year he was ready to make more of a contribution. The Penn State coaching staff first looked at him as a center, then put him at guard. The position was his in 1979 as Penn State went 8-4 and finished with a victory over Tulane in the Liberty Bowl.

"That I was going to play every down was big-time for me," remembers Munchak. "And then the games were all big. Any game I played in was exciting."

The season ended on a down note for Munchak, however. He hurt his knee in the Liberty Bowl and was forced to miss the entire 1980 season, his junior year.

"That was very hard mentally, because I had never been hurt before in my life," Munchak says. "All of a sudden, you're out of the picture and you're not dressed and you're not traveling . . . it's like isolation, it's hard to deal with. It was hard to sit there and watch your friends play and not be part of it."

Munchak was determined to come back for his senior year in 1981. He worked hard at rehab, just as hard as he had worked to be a good football player. By the time the new season rolled around, he was back in the lineup.

The Nittany Lions opened the season ranked No. 5 in the country. After winning their first five games, they had vaulted to No. 1. They still held that ranking after a victory over West Virginia when they traveled down to Miami. The game was played in pouring rain, and Miami upset Penn State 17-14 to knock the Nittany Lions out of the No. 1 spot. Pitt took over the top spot. The Panthers were still there when Penn State, now No. 11, came calling. Munchak remembers the game vividly.

"We played them on Thanksgiving, and they had Dan Marino, and they jumped out 14-0."

But then Penn State rallied.

"Quarterback Todd Blackledge had a huge day, and we hammered them."

Final: Penn State 48, Pitt 14.

"That was a huge win, because we returned the favor of what happened to us in Miami, getting knocked out of number one. So that was a lot of fun. The last game with Pitt, that was the nice way to go out, because that was such a big rivalry then."

Penn State closed out the season with a 26-10 victory over Southern Cal in the Fiesta Bowl to finish at 10-2 and number three in the polls. It had been quite a season for the Nittany Lions, who also beat Notre Dame in winning their last three games. Earlier in the year, they had defeated a ranked Nebraska team as well.

"It was a great finish, but we were disappointed because we thought we had a chance to be number one," Munchak says. "We thought we had some great, great talent on that team between the seniors and juniors, and we blew a great opportunity that year."

Mike Munchak is the offensive line coach for the Tennessee Titans.
Photo courtesy of the Tennessee Titans

Munchak, who had been redshirted in his junior year because of his injury, had a year of football eligibility left at Penn State. He decided to forego it. He was anxious to get started on a pro career and didn't want to chance another injury. More importantly, he had finished his academic requirements (call it the Joe Paterno Rule) and wanted to graduate with his classmates.

"I kind of wanted to go out with my class, with my guys that I came in with. We had a great relationship with that group, and as much as I liked the other guys that were still there, I liked the fact of coming in with that group. We were all real good buddies, and I had an opportunity to leave with them."

Next stop: the Houston Oilers. Munchak was the first offensive lineman chosen, eighth player overall, in the 1982 NFL draft.

For the next 12 years, he was a standout on an offensive line that became one of the best in pro football. In just his third season in the NFL, the Scranton, Pennsylvania, native was named to the first of his seven all-star teams.

He became a force as the Oilers blossomed from an also-ran to a consistent playoff team. For seven straight years from 1987-93, the Oilers didn't miss the playoffs.

"When I came [to the Oilers], the team was very old," says Munchak. "They had traded away a lot of draft picks for a while when they got Earl Campbell. So when I came in, it was the first draft class they had in quite some time."

The Oilers were starting to rebuild, and Munchak was a part of that.

"For four years we didn't win many games, but we had a lot of good draft picks and we built a great team because of that."

Munchak retired after the 1993 season after playing 159 games in the NFL. He joined the Oilers' coaching staff and as the offensive line coach and remained in that position when the team moved to Tennessee in 1997.

In 2001, the Hall of Fame came calling for the father of two daughters. The Hall had found a spot for him.

Not bad for a guy who had a hard time finding a position on his college football team.

KIRK BOWMAN

"It was my 15 minutes of fame," Kirk Bowman says.

In this case, the 15 minutes have lasted a lot longer than Bowman ever imagined.

"It keeps on living," the onetime Penn State tight end says, sounding slightly amazed. "It's a lot of fun. I was fortunate to be in the right place at the right time."

Bowman is talking about the two catches that he made in Penn State's 1982 game against Nebraska. They were the only catches he made all year. And both went for touchdowns in a stunning 27-24 victory over Nebraska. Penn State would go on to win its first national championship, and Bowman would go on to live in the memories of Nittany Lion fans, not to mention Nebraska fans.

At Penn State, Bowman's legacy lifted him to cult hero status. At Nebraska, he was more like the villain.

"Every now and then I'll see a Nebraska fan and they're so good about it," Bowman says. "Nebraska fans in my mind are just some of the top fans in the country. And it's fun to go up and tell them who I am, because just about everybody who's from Nebraska knows who I am."

Talk about destiny. Bowman, who now lives in Texas and works in the health care field, was destined to play football for Penn State. The native Pennsylvanian grew up a Penn State fan, mainly because his father played there. Wayne Bowman was a center for the 1962-63 teams.

"As long as I could remember, even when they had the bleachers in the end zone, I used to sit in the bleachers there in the south end zone, and watch John Cappelletti," Kirk Bowman says. "And it was just very, very special for me, running out on the field the first time as a player. And then I think about winning the national championship—the first one—and knowing my team was the group that was finally able to win that one. It was good for the history, it was good for the program, it was great for Joe Paterno."

Bowman was a tight end at Mechanicsburg (Pennsylvania) High school when recruited by Penn State, but he was tried at several different positions when he got to University Park. Finally he wound up back at tight end. Bowman played behind first-string tight end Mike McCloskey, except when they were both used in the two tight-end set. Even then, McCloskey was the main receiver. Bowman's role was usually as a blocker, but he didn't mind.

"I liked the physical aspect of it," Bowman says. "It's a fun position."

KIRK BOWMAN

Years lettered: 1980, 1981, 1982 and 1983
Position: Tight end
Accomplishments: Most remembered for two touchdown catches he made in the 1982 Nebraska game.

Bowman didn't know how much fun it was going to be, though, especially when Nebraska came to town. It was a match-up of Top Ten powers—Nebraska was No. 2 and Penn State, No. 8—and would go down as a game for the ages at University Park.

Bowman made his presence felt right away when he caught a 14-yard pass from Todd Blackledge for a touchdown to give the Lions an early 7-0 lead. Penn State led most of the way, but the Huskers battled back and eventually went ahead, 24-21, with just 78 seconds left.

The Lions took over and needed to move the ball 65 yards for the winning points.

"I actually started that drive," Bowman recalls. "I don't know why. For some reason, I was in for Mike. I think they ran a screen play or something. I remember being in the huddle at the start of that drive, and Todd Blackledge just came into the huddle very calm. There was absolutely no panic. Blackledge said, 'Look, we've practiced this every day in practice. We're marching down this field and we're going to score.' Then he called the play, broke the huddle. Nobody panicked, and boom, we started down the field."

Making good use of the clock, Blackledge led the Lions downfield. In nine plays, they were on the Nebraska 17-yard line with 27 seconds left. Blackledge then connected with McCloskey, putting the ball at the 2 with just nine seconds left. Then Paterno did something that surprised Bowman. He had him switch positions with McCloskey.

"Normally, Mike's on the strong side and the second tight end comes in on the weak side," Bowman recalls. "But evidentally, the coaches saw something in the films that made them want to flip us. So for that play and that play only, Mike McCloskey and I actually flipped positions. I went over to the strong-side tight end, and he went over to the weak side."

The play was designed to go to the weak-side tight end, in this case, McCloskey.

"The other tight end's job was to just get in behind the linebackers and find a hole," says Bowman, referring to himself. "For that whole game, it was almost impossible to release off the line to the outside. Nebraska just wasn't letting us get outside. On that play I think Mike either got hung up or got covered real quick. For some reason, no one seemed to be covering me trailing across the back."

Blackledge spotted Bowman open in the back of the end zone. He fired in his direction.

"It was a low pass and it's something that we do, believe or not, at the beginning of practice every day," Bowman says. "You actually practice catching low balls. And it was one where I had to get both arms underneath the ball and was literally six to nine inches off the ground when it got to me."

TOUCHDOWN!

"On my first touchdown catch, there was a little bit of green between the end zones," Bowman says. "The second one I was right in the very back of the end zone, because there wasn't any room left."

The catch gave the Lions a thrilling comeback victory, 27-24, and proved to be a determining factor in winning their first national championship. The following week, Penn State was stunned by Alabama. Many of the Penn State players were down after that 42-21 drubbing, thinking the national championship had been lost.

Joel Coles wasn't one of them. He stood up in the locker room and gave an impassioned speech. In essence, he said: "It's not over. We're going to win the rest of our games. And we're going to have a chance to win the national championship."

"It was a pretty moving after-game speech," Bowman remembers. "It wasn't Joe Paterno or anybody who really made a speech that set the tone for the rest of the season. It was Joel Coles. That was just a huge, huge turning point where we rededicated ourselves. First things first, we had to win the rest of our games."

The Lions did, and by the end of the season, they finished No. 1 after beating Georgia in the Sugar Bowl. The poll voters took into account Penn State's tough schedule in making them the top team.

"One of the neatest things, looking back and reflecting on it, we were the first team to win a national championship [at Penn State]," Bowman says. "But you know what, there were a lot of people before us who really laid the groundwork for that, the teams that went 12-0 and didn't get it.

"Even the team the year before, that team was playing so well at the end of the season, you could probably make an argument it was playing better than anyone in the country."

Bowman refers to the 1981 Penn State team that finished the regular season with victories over Notre Dame and then a Pittsburgh team that was ranked No. 1 in the country. Then the Lions beat Southern Cal in the Fiesta Bowl as Curt Warner outshone Heisman Trophy winner Marcus Allen.

"If you look at the NFL players from that football team, it's shocking," says Bowman. "From my sophomore year, there was Mike Munchak, Sean Farrell, Jim Romano. Obviously the skill players were there, Todd Blackledge, Curt Warner, Gregg Garrity, and all those guys. I think that whole starting offense almost went pro.

"The last three, four games of the season, that was certainly as good a football team as the next year when we won the national championship."

In Bowman's senior year, 1983, the Lions lost their first three games of the season. But then they turned things around, losing only once in their last 10 games. They finished up with a victory over Washington in the Aloha Bowl.

"I saved my best block for the last play," Bowman says. "We were near the goal line, and I just remember blocking the defensive end. I put him on his back, outside the end zone. I drove him all the way through the end zone. I thought, yeah, that's a good way to end a career. And I never got to see it on film, because when you're a senior, you're gone."

Following the season, Bowman started the process familiar to most seniors in college: interviewing for jobs.

"Since I was a small kid, I was always helping out and working in some aspect of the grocery business," Bowman says. "My father was in charge of operations for a group of convenience stores called Handy Markets. To me, the best thing that I ever could have been was a consumer salesperson."

Bowman ended up taking a job with the Hershey Chocolate Company and started out as a territorial sales rep in Florida. He later worked in medical sales and eventually found his way to Texas to work in sales in the health care field. Among other things, Bowman's company, Paper Pack Products, manufactures a life-saving device called a "Rapid Infuser" that warms blood in I.V. fluids during trauma situations.

"And we have letter after letter after letter stating that if it wasn't for this piece of equipment, this person wouldn't be alive," Bowman says. "And that's just a small piece of our business. It's a $1.1 billion-dollar company."

Bowman and his wife, Nancy, have three children and enjoy living in Texas. There is still a big part of Pennsylvania in Bowman, though—particularly the part of his years at Penn State.

"To be part of the program was just an absolute dream come true," Bowman says.

GREGG GARRITY

Gregg Garrity lives on a street called "Seldom Seen Road." That's ironic, because more people than you can imagine have seen Garrity's historic catch against Georgia in the 1983 Sugar Bowl. There were the 78,124 fans at the Louisiana Superdome the night of the game, the millions who watched on national TV and, of course, the hundreds of thousands of readers who saw his catch immortalized on the cover of *Sports Illustrated*.

When discussing important events in Penn State's football history, you don't need to say any more than "The Catch" to many Nittany Lion fans from the '80s, and they'll know what you're talking about. After all, Garrity's huge catch helped Penn State clinch its first national football championship.

Oddly enough, the sure-handed Garrity didn't start out as a receiver at Penn State. He was basically a defensive back for most of the first year he was there.

"It just so happened that they were thin at that position," Garrity remembers of his freshman year at Penn State in 1979. "So actually I got some playing time in my freshman year up there, playing on special teams, and such."

Garrity, who made the Penn State team as a walk-on before earning a scholarship for his next three years, would go on to play professional football. One of his distinctions: he caught the last touchdown pass thrown by the Pittsburgh Steelers' all-pro quarterback Terry Bradshaw.

"It was a great experience," Garrity says of his time with the Steelers. "Growing up in the Pittsburgh area and actually getting to meet and play with Bradshaw, Franco Harris, and Jack Lambert was cool. I could go down the list of guys I played with—a lot of the legends."

Going to Penn State for his first look at the campus, there was no way Garrity could have envisioned himself playing for the Pittsburgh Steelers. Or even playing for Penn State, for that matter.

"The only reason I went up to Penn State was through my dad," Garrity says. "My dad was the first person ever recruited by Paterno, back when he was an assistant coach with Rip Engle. Other than that, I definitely wouldn't have even gone up there. They looked at me, and my size was basically my big problem, because I was about 5-10, maybe 135 to 140 pounds."

Jim Garrity was co-captain of the 1954 Penn State team. But that didn't help Gregg Garrity too much as Paterno guided him and his father around the football facilities. Gregg felt totally out of place.

GREGG GARRITY

Years lettered: 1980, 1981 and 1982
Position: Wide receiver
Accomplishments: Led the Lions in catches in 1981
with 23 for 415 yards, but greatest of all was the
TD catch he made in the 1983 Sugar Bowl, which
clinched Penn State's first national championship.

"It was kind of interesting," Garrity remembers. "Joe showed us the weight room and stuff, and Bruce Clark and Matt Millen were in the weight room. I was a 140-pound kid and these guys were houses. I thought, 'You've got to be kidding me.' I was as big as one of Bruce's legs. He was a specimen. That's when you have to sit down and think, 'Man, what am I going to do here?'"

Even though Penn State opened the door for Garrity, he still had to show his worth. Except for missing a couple of games with a knee injury suffered in practice, he dressed for every game as a freshman.

"I was happy just to be there and did what I was told," he says. "I had a no-lose situation. There was nothing expected of me, by myself, or anybody. So I just went in and did my best, and whatever happened, happened."

Here's exactly what happened: Garrity eventually blossomed into one of Penn State's top receivers in the early '80s. In 1981, he led the Lions in receiving when he averaged 18 yards a catch.

That team went 10-2 and finished strong with victories over Notre Dame and top-ranked Pittsburgh. Then the Lions knocked off Southern Cal in the Fiesta Bowl.

"I still think that team was actually a better team than it was in my senior year," Garrity says.

The 1981 Penn State team featured future NFL Hall of Famer Mike Munchak and several other great players. The Lions lost 11 starters from that squad and faced a brutal schedule in 1982 that featured such teams as Pitt, Alabama, Nebraska and Notre Dame—all ranked in the Top 20 in the preseason polls.

Remembering that season, Garrity says:

"A lot of good things happened. The team came together and started clicking at the right time. We'd worked together for three years to get to that point. We just had a lot of trust in each other."

The Lions got off to a 4-0 start, including a momentous win over second-ranked Nebraska. Then came a disheartening 42-21 loss to Alabama. The loss dropped Penn State from No. 3 to No. 8 in the national polls. But the Lions moved back toward the top again with a string of victories. By the end of the regular season, enough teams had fallen by the wayside to allow Penn State to climb to No. 2 and set up a showdown with top-ranked Georgia for the national title.

Penn State rushed to an early 20-3 lead, only to see Georgia respond behind Heisman Trophy winner Herschel Walker. The Bulldogs cut the Lions' lead to 20-17 in the third quarter.

Early in the fourth quarter Todd Blackledge fired a 47-yard touchdown pass to Garrity, who made a fully extended diving catch in the end zone. It gave Penn State a 27-17 lead and helped the Lions to withstand a late score by Georgia. Final: Penn State 27, Georgia 23.

Garrity recalls that Penn State ran the play a lot that year.

"Basically, it was just four guys [as receivers]. The running back and tight end, Curt Warner and Mike McCloskey, ran basically down the hashes and Kenny Jackson on one side and myself on the other just ran fly routes on the outside. I was on the left side.

"We had all seams covered, and someone should be open. All year ... I never really got the ball. But they happened to be in the right defense on that play, when we called it, and fortunately I was the one who was open."

Garrity also made some other important catches in the game with four receptions for 116 yards.

"The most important one was probably the last one, which is only like a six- or seven-yard route that was on third down that got us the first down to keep Herschel Walker and their offense off the field," Garrity says.

In the course of the victory, the Lions' defense didn't let Walker take over the game. As a matter of fact, Warner outplayed the Heisman winner.

"We had all the confidence in our defense," Garrity says. "There may not have been any superstars on defense but, boy, they made some great plays together."

It was a great way for Garrity to close his Penn State career—a national championship and his fourth bowl victory in four tries.

The Sugar Bowl victory over Georgia was one of many good memories for Garrity.

"I think everything started with the USC game," says Garrity, recalling the 26-10 victory over Southern Cal in the 1982 Fiesta Bowl. "I had a touchdown in that one against Joey Browner, who was one of the top defensive backs in the country."

And like the catch against Georgia, this was also a long pass thrown by Blackledge.

"It seemed like from that point on, my confidence level and just everything sort of changed," Garrity said.

After school, Garrity was drafted by the Steelers. He played in Pittsburgh for about a year and a half before he was released. Just when the Steelers thought about bringing him back because of a shortage of offensive players, Garrity was picked up by the Philadelphia Eagles.

"That was the weekend ironically that Kenny Jackson got hurt in Philadelphia, so then they picked me right up," recalls Garrity. "I was there for six and a half years."

When he first got to Philadelphia, Garrity was not happy. Then things changed.

"I didn't know many people," he says. "But actually it became a pretty good situation in Philadelphia. I really enjoyed playing there. The fans are a little crazy, but they also know their football. And if you do your job and work hard at it, they're really good to you. It's just when you slack off a little bit that they're pretty tough."

During his years with the Eagles, Garrity became involved with the Special Olympics. In the summer of 1992, he was made honorary chairman of the Pennsylvania Summer Special Olympics. He considers it one of the highlights of his life.

"A lot of people didn't give these special athletes a chance to do anything in the world, but through determination and hard work, they give their all," Garrity told a reporter for the *Penn State Collegian*. "I see a lot of them in me. People told me I was definitely too small to play football, but I went against the odds and was lucky enough to be one of the select few to play professional football."

After retiring from the NFL, Garrity opened a construction business near his hometown of Bradfordwoods, Pennsylvania.

"I do a lot of home renovations," says Garrity, who has two children with his wife, Linda.

The business is called, fittingly, "All Hands on Deck."

Wouldn't you just know that a sure-handed receiver like Garrity would have the word hands somewhere in the title of his business?

MARK BATTAGLIA

Mark Battaglia likes to call it "A Tale of Two Sugar Bowls."

"Against Bear Bryant in 1978 we just couldn't get it over from three yards out," Battaglia says. "Then in the Sugar Bowl in '82, we beat Vince Dooley and Herschel Walker. It was a remarkable stretch."

Battaglia was a freshman watching from the sidelines when Penn State lost the national championship to Alabama in the 1979 Sugar Bowl. In the 1983 Sugar Bowl, he was a fifth-year senior when the Lions won the championship by beating Georgia in the showdown of No. 1 and No. 2 in New Orleans. From 1978-82, Penn State had a remarkable 50-10 record against some of the toughest competition in the country. The 1982 season was especially tough with such ranked opponents as Nebraska, Alabama, Notre Dame, Pitt and Georgia on the schedule.

"One of my teammates, Bill Contz, sent me a report that the schedule was the toughest of any national championship team," Battaglia says. "That went back to 1977 when they first started keeping track of this. It was an unbelievable schedule."

Also hard to believe: Penn State won the national title despite an imperfect record after so many seasons of missing with perfect records. The Lions suffered a mid-season thrashing by Alabama and finished at 11-1.

"How ironic, huh?" Battaglia muses. "Maybe that's what you have to do, lose one game to win it."

One month after the Sugar Bowl, Battaglia found himself in another hard-to-believe situation: in a United States Football League training camp.

"You talk about, 'I can't believe it.' To go from winning the national championship to being in camp a month later. I was barely sober by then, and I was not particularly in the right frame of mind," he recalls. "I was drafted by the Philadelphia Stars. So I went from winning the national championship on Bourbon Street to a camp with Jim Mora, who's an ex-Marine who is noted for his unbelievable hitting and intensity. That guy was just crazy. Making $5 a day in camp was weird, too. It was like the diamond mines in South Africa."

Joe Paterno's camps were a little different. Paterno was one of the main reasons Battaglia went to Penn State, along with the Lions' far-reaching schedule. Battaglia, an all-state linebacker and center at Upper St. Clair High School in Pittsburgh, was highly recruited. After a visit to Northwestern, he was convinced he was going there. Then he thought the same after visiting Virginia. Finally, he decided on Penn State.

"Joe took my dad out for a Friday night," Battaglia remembers. "After the dinner, he took him over to his house and there was never a question after that. He is quite the charmer."

MARK BATTAGLIA

Years lettered: 1980, 1981 and 1982
Position: Offensive lineman

Battaglia didn't find it easy making the starting lineup at Penn State, though.

"Joe buried me [on the offensive line] and I don't think he ever expected to see me again. It took, really, three and a half years to be a factor. I played my fourth year, played a decent amount. I didn't start, but I played the entire second half against USC in the Fiesta Bowl when Jim Romano got hurt.

"Up to then, it was the most important playing time of my career and really gave me a lot of confidence going into what would be my fifth year. But I had to wait a long time. I never stopped believing in what I could do, and I never stopped working to get to where I needed to be."

Say the same for the whole Penn State team in 1982, especially following that 42-21 loss to Alabama in Birmingham in the fifth game of the season. Going into the game, Penn State had been ranked No. 3 in the country and Alabama No. 4.

"We went down there and just had one of those games where we didn't do anything right," Battaglia recalls. "It was very uncharacteristic. We couldn't control their defensive ends, and we were having trouble running the ball. We blocked our own punt with our personal protector. I don't think I've seen that happen to anybody since. So, it was just one of those things that started and we went downhill."

The players were naturally down after that loss. But then something positive happened in the locker room.

"Joel Coles, our fullback at the time, gave one of the most inspirational speeches of the year," Battaglia says. "He was really an inspirational leader, a very fiery guy, and he just laid it out: 'You know, what are we doing here? Are we going to let this ruin our season? Or refocus and beat the rest of the schedule, and keep going ahead?' He really gave a great speech.

"We came back Monday with a purpose. And it turned out, in hindsight, that was the turning point for our season, that speech in a Birmingham, Alabama, locker room by Joel Coles."

The Lions, who had been dropped to No. 8 after the loss to Alabama, won their last six games of the season to climb back to No. 2 and set up a meeting with Georgia in the 1983 Sugar Bowl.

"The Sugar Bowl was like a dream," Battaglia says. "The whole thing was like a dream. It seemed like it was in slow motion to me. The atmosphere in the Superdome was something I'd never really seen. The longer you got into the game, it was like a haze in there . . . a haze of smoke. I guess people were smoking. But we were very confident all week long and during the game."

Running back Curt Warner had a great game, outplaying the Heisman-winning Walker, and Gregg Garrity made a spectacular diving TD catch in the fourth quarter for the decisive points. The Lions went on to their first national championship with a 27-23 victory.

Garrity's catch was immortalized on the cover of *Sports Illustrated*. Another picture worth a thousand words: the Penn State players, their index fingers raised in the "No. 1" sign, carrying Paterno off the field.

"I was right behind Joe. I may have had a hand on him, holding him up," Battaglia says.

Mark Battaglia is a financial adviser in Pittsburgh.
He and his wife, Diane, have three children.
Photo courtesy of Mark Battaglia

Next stop for Battaglia: training camp with the Philadelphia Stars of the newly organized United States Football League (USFL). That lasted three weeks, or until the Stars signed a center by the name of Bart Oates.

"That made me expendable, and they traded me to the Birmingham Stallions," Battaglia says. "You talk about going from the absolute pinnacle at the Sugar Bowl to within a month and a half having to face the proposition of going to Birmingham—it was disheartening.

"The reason I wanted to play for the Stars was because it was close to Pittsburgh. And to go to Birmingham, the site of one of my worst experiences in football, I almost quit."

In retrospect, Battaglia is glad he didn't.

"They turned out to be three of the best years of my life, playing for Rollie Dotsch," Battaglia says. "Rollie is the type of guy people would run through walls for. He was such a guy's guy."

The USFL had announced its formation in 1982 as a spring league and battled the more established NFL for players, fans and media attention. Herschel Walker, the Heisman Trophy winner who had played for Georgia against Penn State in the 1983 Sugar Bowl, left college a year early to sign with the New Jersey Generals. Other established NFL players came over to play in the new league, which featured not only big names, but name owners such as free-spending and high-spirited Donald Trump.

In the first year, the league, with teams in NFL strongholds such as the New York metropolitan area, Philadelphia, Boston, Oakland and Los Angeles, averaged more than

25,000 fans a game. The Stallions, actually, had one of the better teams in the upstart league. They featured running back Joe Cribbs, quarterback Cliff Stoudt and receiver Jim Smith. Under Dotsch, Birmingham had a 36-18 record over three years.

"We had a lot of success in Birmingham. We had the second best record in USFL history behind the Stars," Battaglia recalls. "We just could never beat the Stars. We beat 'em two times in the regular season the third and final year of the league, and then lost to them in the playoffs."

Interestingly enough, the Stars were led by quarterback Chuck Fusina, who had graduated from Penn State just a few years before Battaglia.

After three seasons, the USFL made big plans to move to a fall schedule and challenge the NFL head on. The new league also took the NFL to court in an antitrust suit, claiming the older league had an iron-grip monopoly on football. The USFL "won" the case, but lost the war.

"It was terrible," Battaglia says, "but it shows you how powerful the NFL is. It's the most powerful monopoly in the world. Donald Trump tried to take them on and we lost.

"We won the lawsuit claiming that they monopolized the television contracts. Three women on the jury wanted to give us three hundred million dollars, which would have been trebled to six hundred million, and the other three women on the jury couldn't decide what the damages were. So they compromised it to a dollar. It was an unbelievable travesty of justice."

After that, Battaglia "got on with my life's work. I became a financial adviser and have been doing that ever since."

Battaglia works with Merrill Lynch, which has strong Penn State ties. Bill Schreyer, former chairman of the board of Merrill Lynch, is also a former chairman of the board at Penn State and a Penn State graduate. Penn State has received a number of generous gifts from Schreyer, including $30 million to help finance a business school in his name.

Battaglia's ties to Penn State also run deep.

"It's been 23 years since you've played, and everyone still associates you with the national championship team," Battaglia says of himself and his former teammates. "Coming to Penn State was the best decision I ever made. Something that happened 23 years ago is still very much a part of my life."

He considers his story "a hard-work-pays-off-type story, overachieving to some degree."

"You stick to it, and every once in a while you're rewarded," says Battaglia, who has three children with his wife, Diane, whom he met at Penn State. "I've been rewarded for 23 years."

ERIC HAMILTON

Third and long. Every college football team has found itself in such a desperate situation. It's more desperate when you're battling from behind. And just imagine how much desperation there is when the game is for no less than the national championship?

Penn State found itself in this tight spot in the 1987 Fiesta Bowl against Miami. The Nittany Lions were third-and-12 in the second quarter and trailing Miami 7-0. They had to make a first down or punt the ball to the Hurricanes and give them the opportunity to build on their lead.

Football reasoning dictated that Penn State quarterback John Shaffer call a pass play. The Hurricanes knew it. The broadcasters knew it. Every fan in the stadium knew it. Eric Hamilton felt confident that if the ball was thrown to him, he could get his team the needed yardage.

"I wasn't a speed burner," Hamilton says, reflecting on the national championship game nearly 20 years later. "But as my career wound up at Penn State, I was beginning to think of myself as a possession-type receiver, someone who could make the clutch catch and keep a drive going."

Hamilton, now in private business in the Cleveland area, took his position when the huddle broke and waited for the snap. Seems Hamilton had been pointing toward this big moment on the football field nearly all his life. Or since he fell in love with Penn State. Hamilton had played tailback and receiver at Hawken, a small private school in Cleveland. For as long as he could remember, he always wanted to catch passes.

Even so, Hamilton wasn't so sure he could play big-time football at a school like Penn State. His high school coach believed in him, though. He set up a tryout for Hamilton.

"In my mind, I'm not thinking of going to a school like Penn State. But as the days go on, and I'm participating in the drills, I'm thinking, I'm catching the ball pretty good. Maybe I'm one of the faster kids there."

When Hamilton was asked to run the 40-yard dash and was told by a coach, "You've got some nice speed," Hamilton started to re-think his situation.

"Probably the last couple of days, it starts to dawn on me this is more than, 'I'm here to have fun.' They're looking at me to give me a scholarship to play football!" recalls Hamilton. "I think going in with the mindset I had, this little naïve mindset, helped me in some shape or form to get noticed by the coaching staff there. There was no pressure on me."

Welcome to Penn State, Eric. And welcome to red-shirt status.

"There was a large core of us [red-shirted]. We came in as freshmen and experienced the national championship right away," says Hamilton.

ERIC HAMILTON

Years lettered: 1985 and 1986
Position: Wide receiver
Accomplishments: His key catch in the 1987
Fiesta Bowl helped the Lions beat Miami
for their second national title in five years.

Eric Hamilton and wife Patty have two children. He owns a sign-making business in Ohio and works with the Cleveland Touchdown Club Charities to raise scholarship money for student athletes.
Photo courtesy of Eric Hamilton

That was the 1982 season, when Penn State beat Georgia in the Sugar Bowl 27-23 to win the national title. Hamilton, and the other freshman, thought that playing in a national championship game would be a given for the next four years. But, as Hamilton recalls, "some people graduated, and we had a couple of down years. We quit, frankly. We stunk up the place."

A 7-4-1 season and a victory over Washington in the Aloha Bowl would be a good year for a lot of teams. Not for Penn State. Not after winning the national championship. Then a 6-5 season followed in 1984. And worse, no bowl.

"We had a couple down years in there," Hamilton says. "If we lost two games during the time we were there, you thought the world came to an end. You didn't want to go to class, you didn't want to go to a party, you didn't want to go to practice, you didn't want to see any part of Joe Paterno."

Things suddenly changed in 1985. The Lions went 11-0 and found themselves in the Orange Bowl against Oklahoma playing for the national championship. They lost the game but gained some motivation.

"We were thinking we were coming back and winning the whole thing the next year," Hamilton says. "Deep down inside, I think each of us knew. We didn't have to talk about it. We just knew that we were going to work hard and get back to that game again."

They were even more confident during the 1986 season after beating second-ranked Alabama on the road, 23-3, to extend their record to 7-0.

"That was the best regular-season game I experienced at Penn State," Hamilton says. "We were well prepared, and we kept them out of the end zone. We had a senior-laden team and just did a job on them. And you really knew it in the locker room after the game. It was like we won the national championship. We couldn't have been more excited."

Penn State moved up in the polls from No. 6 to No. 2. That's where they finished the season, behind top-ranked Miami. That set up a national championship showdown in a battle of unbeatens between No. 1 and No. 2.

Falling behind 7-0 in the second quarter, the Lions came back with a drive of their own. But the Lions suddenly lost yardage and faced a third and 12.

"Miami was in what we called Two-Deep Coverage," Hamilton recalls. "You had the two safeties playing deep in a zone coverage and the two corners were playing man to man. Miami played man because they could. They had the athletes to do that. They had the speed.

"So when your number's called in a situation like that, you're saying, 'Okay, I know what I have to run—I have to run a post pattern.' I just wanted to get a little bit of separation so that John was able to find me."

Hamilton found the space he needed, and Shaffer found him—for a 23-yard gain!

"Now we've got a little confidence. We've got a little something going here."

And so Penn State did. Thanks to Hamilton's drive-saving catch, the Lions tied the game and went on to beat Miami 14-10 for their second national championship in four years.

After college, Hamilton had a tryout with the Seattle Seahawks as a walk-on.

"I knew I had to make the team, and I quite frankly didn't perform," Hamilton says. "I think part of it was because of the pressure of knowing that this wasn't fun anymore, this was a job now."

Hamilton grew up in a household that had stressed education over athletics.

"I looked at things a little differently. So by the time I got to professional football, I couldn't believe I was there. And that's not the kind of attitude you have to have to play in the NFL. I was in Seattle and I was thinking, this is a different ball game. I didn't have a whole lot of speed for the next level. I didn't go into that situation with a lot of confidence."

Then he got a call from the Seahawks: they were going to waive him.

"At the time it was kind of tough. And I knew then I wasn't the type who was going to go chasing. I knew at that time my football life as I knew it was over."

Hamilton came back home to Cleveland and worked for IMG, the superpower group that supplies agents for athletes.

"I wanted to stay close to the sports industry and be an agent," Hamilton said. "I did that for a couple of years, but I wasn't too crazy about that."

Hamilton then worked as a marketing representative for IBM before going back to grad school for his master's degree. He spent several years in finance before starting his own business in the sign-making industry. Hamilton purchased a franchise from a national chain called "Signs By Tomorrow," and planned to run that business full time. Meanwhile, he has also remained close to football as a board member for The Cleveland Touchdown Club Charities. The motto of the organization is, "Give Kids a Sporting Chance." The group raises money for scholarships for student athletes.

Hamilton also coached some high school football for a while.

"I was an assistant working with the wide-outs and defensive backs trying to instill what I learned from my experiences at Penn State," says Hamilton, who has a son and daughter with his wife, Patty. "I did that for four years in my spare time. Then my spare time ran out."

Interestingly, the slogan of Hamilton's new sign-making business is: "Imagine it. We can do it."

Sounds like something he learned on the football fields of Penn State.

BOB WHITE

This is a story about second chances, and making them count. A story of determination, redemption and fulfillment. A story of inspiration.

It is the story of Bob White and the 1986 Penn State football team.

It all started in 1982 when White was a freshman at Penn State, part of one of Joe Paterno's best recruiting classes. White and many of his classmates had been red-shirted. They played on the "foreign team," practicing against the eventual national champions.

When White wasn't working hard on the field, he was working just as hard in the classroom. He had taken a red-shirt year as a freshman to fulfill academic requirements. He did, with the help of Sue Paterno, the coach's wife. White had overcome sub-par high school grades to make the most of a second chance. Now he was ready to play football as a sophomore, with still four years of eligibility left if he wanted them.

The story continues with the rest of the Penn State team. The Nittany Lions had gone 11-0 in 1985 before a 25-10 loss to Oklahoma in the Orange Bowl. It cost Penn State the national championship. Now comes the part about the Nittany Lions' second chance as a team.

"When you work that hard and get that close you can taste something—that taste doesn't leave your mouth," White says. "At that point, a lot of the red-shirt guys who could have left ended up coming back for that fifth year because we realized that we could get it done."

White, a defensive lineman, was one of 15 fifth-year seniors who came back to University Park for another season.

"We came up short in the Orange Bowl," White says. "We wanted to give it another shot."

That meant sweating it out in off-season workouts, spring practice, and then months of practice before playing another game. Then came the hard part: winning every one of their games, including the bowl game at the end against one of the country's top teams.

No problem. This was a team on a mission. And as one of the co-captains, White was ready to lead them. Linebacker Shane Conlan, fullback Steve Smith and quarterback John Shaffer were named captains along with White by their teammates. White, as he had done all through high school and college, would lead by example. He had always been a hard worker who could play just about anywhere he was asked. At Freeport High School in western Pennsylvania north of Pittsburgh, he was a running back as a sophomore, and then a fullback and linebacker in his junior and senior years.

When White visited Penn State, he developed an immediate, almost mystical, attachment to the school.

BOB WHITE

Years lettered: 1983, 1984, 1985 and 1986
Position: Defensive lineman
Accomplishments: Collected 18 career sacks.

"My initial gut reaction to the place when I first visited was very positive," he says. "I thought the people at Penn State were very sincere about their intentions, in terms of helping me achieve the things I wanted to achieve."

Getting his classwork in order was one thing. Sharpening his football skills was another. White ended up playing defensive tackle and defensive end—and he played those positions like he was born to them. He seemed to be everywhere on the field when a key defensive play was needed.

Ask Doug Flutie, the great Boston College quarterback, who was forced to fumble deep in Penn State territory by White in a crucial spot in the teams' 1984 meeting. The Lions held on to win, 37-30. Or ask Syracuse's Roland Grimes, forced into a fumble by White, who then recovered, in the 1985 game. The play, late in the game, helped the Nittany Lions prevail, 24-20. Or ask Maryland quarterback Don Henning in 1986. Twice White forced Henning into crucial turnovers to help the Lions hold off the Terps, 17-15.

Meanwhile, White and his elite freshmen classmates were growing together into a formidable football team. It didn't happen overnight, though.

"We had some lukewarm stretches there," White recalls. "1983 and '84 were winning seasons, but not your typical Penn State seasons."

Penn State went 8-4-1 in 1983, winning the Aloha Bowl over Washington, 13-10. The Nittany Lions finished the season ranked as the No. 17 team in the country. In 1984, they finished at 6-5 and out of the rankings before a comeback in 1985. The Nittany Lions began that season unranked, but by the end of the year they were No. 1. Then came the Oklahoma disaster in the Orange Bowl and a renewed determination.

In 1986, there were plenty of close calls along the way. It wasn't a season; it was a survival test—especially against Notre Dame. Notre Dame led 13-10 in the third quarter when Penn State rallied to take an 11-point lead. The Fighting Irish closed to 24-19 late in the game. Then with a minute to go, Notre Dame was second-and-goal from the 9-yard line.

Enter Bob White. Enter into the Notre Dame backfield, that is. White shot through from his left tackle position to pin Notre Dame quarterback Steve Beuerlein for a nine-yard loss. The sack moved the Fighting Irish back to the 18-yard line and pretty much sacked their chances for victory.

After Penn State held on for a 24-19 victory, Notre Dame coach Lou Holtz told the *Washington Post*: "The most critical play was the sack, because going from the 18 is a lot different than going from the 9."

With a victory over Pitt, Penn State finished the season unbeaten and headed to a bowl game once more with an 11-0 record and a chance to win the national championship. There the second-ranked Nittany Lions faced the top-ranked Miami Hurricanes in the Fiesta Bowl.

"There was no need for pollsters, or anyone," White says. "It was one and two and if you got it done, you were champion. And it was a great position to be in."

A second chance for Penn State, and a last chance for a big part of the team. Twenty-nine seniors, some red-shirted and others in their fifth year, would complete their eligibility. Seventeen of them were starters.

"Our fate was completely in our hands," White says.

So what did the Lions do? They simply picked off five passes thrown by Heisman Trophy winner Vinny Testaverde. Shane Conlan made one of the biggest interceptions with his second of the night in the fourth quarter. Conlan raced to the Miami six, setting up a touchdown run by D.J. Dozier that gave Penn State a 14-10 lead.

Testaverde wasn't finished, though. With about three minutes left, he marched the Canes deep into Penn State territory. At that point, the Penn State defense wouldn't break. It wouldn't even bend. White and the rest of the defensive line kept coming up with big plays—earning a sack and forcing an errant pass. Finally, there were just 18 seconds left. Testaverde went back to pass. He spotted a receiver in the left side of the end zone. Just as Testaverde threw, Pete Giftopolous threw himself in the line of fire and picked off the pass.

Game over. Penn State 14, Miami 10.

The national championship belonged to Penn State for the second time in five seasons. White remembered how his emotions washed over him on the field following one of Penn State's biggest victories.

"It was just a great culmination of two years—actually the whole stretch—but particularly the last two years and how much hard work had gone into it, and the fact that we had fought ourselves back to a position where our fate was completely in our hands, which was perfect."

White had a try at a pro football career, first with the San Francisco 49ers and then the Cleveland Browns. It didn't work out.

"I'm not disappointed," White says. "I have no regrets. Things couldn't have worked out any better."

He began an administrative career at Penn State in 1989 as a counselor in the Admissions office. During this period, he earned a master's degree in counselor education. In 1992, he was named Director of Legislative Affairs at the Penn State Office of Governmental Affairs.

"Working in admissions and governmental affairs provided me with a solid background," he says. "I was able to learn more about the university and how the university works."

In 1995, White returned to athletics when he was picked to be an assistant for newly named Director of Athletics Tim Curley. White was involved with special projects, including working with the coaching staffs, admissions office and housing office.

White later was an assistant football coach under Paterno, working with special teams.

"From there, I came back to where I am now," says White, currently Penn State director of marketing and operations for suites and club seats and private events at Beaver Stadium.

He likes to think of Penn State as more than a state university, perhaps more like a state of mind.

"It's always been known for its close-knit, family-oriented approach and dealings with people," White says. "And I think anyone who leaves here, that's one of the things they leave with: that sense of family and belonging and being a part of something really special."

Being part of something special is certainly something that White can identify with. That, and making good on a second chance.

Where Have You Gone?

FRANK
GIANNETTI

These days, Frank Giannetti coaches high school football at Toms River North in the general area of his roots in central New Jersey. It could also be called, "Penn State East." Working with young football players, the former Penn State defensive lineman and NFL player applies lessons he learned from his days with the Nittany Lions.

"The kids listen," Giannetti says, "because they know that what I'm asking them to do is basically what I did."

At Penn State, Giannetti worked hard on scout teams as a freshman, playing the part of the varsity's competition from week to week.

"It was an experience being a tight end and having to block Shane Conlan every day in practice," Giannetti says. "Then they moved me to defense, and Tim Manoa was kicking me out on power sweeps. My freshman year in college, I was on the scout team against probably eight or nine guys who played in the NFL. That's why I got better."

Somewhere in his sophomore year at Penn State, Giannetti took over the starting defensive tackle position. No one moved him out of there for the remainder of his college career.

It was not hard to see why. Fighting through adversity—and pain—was simply a matter of personal style for Giannetti. Take the Virginia game that opened the 1989 season, for instance. In the first quarter, Giannetti broke his hand making a tackle. He was taken to the hospital.

"They X-rayed it and put a cast on it," Giannetti says. "I came back and played in the second half."

Giannetti had surgery the next day. He was out one week, but came back and played with a cast.

"By the middle of the season, when it was pretty much healed, I got the cast off and got my hand back," Giannetti remembers. "I was just so excited to use my hands again."

Giannetti had always been considered a "gamer", going back to his high school days. At Toms River East, he played tight end and linebacker. He was recruited by Penn State as "an athlete." Translation: coaches had a tough time finding a position for him.

"Coming out of high school, I was a lot smaller," Giannetti says. "I was about 6-3, 230, so I really didn't know where I was going to play."

When Giannetti got to camp that summer, he was first tried out at tight end. Then, over the next year and a half, he played some fullback and linebacker before being moved to the tackle spot. There Giannetti found himself about the same time that Penn State

FRANK GIANNETTI

Years lettered: 1988, 1989 and 1990
Position: Defensive tackle

was trying to find itself as a team. In 1988, the Lions suffered through a 5-6 season, Joe Paterno's first losing season at Penn State in 23 years.

"We lost a number of close games that year," Giannetti recalls. "I think one of the biggest things, Joe admitted he kind of started letting things get a little lax.

"And that off season, I'll never forget, when we got back to Penn State, he read a three- or four-page list of rules in our first team meeting. It was everything from not wearing sweats to class to not wearing hats in classrooms. No walkmans on buses. He didn't want any beards and stuff. Your hair couldn't be too long. It was just a lot of different things. And that off-season conditioning was one of the ones that really stands out in my mind, because we just worked our butts off."

So, guess what? The Lions restored order with an 8-3-1 season in 1989 that included a 50-39 victory over Brigham Young in the Holiday Bowl.

The Lions started the 1990 season with a Top 25 ranking and high hopes. Close losses to Texas and Southern Cal at the start knocked the Lions out of the polls but didn't knock them off their game. All they did was win seven in a row, including a shutout of Alabama on the road, to move back into the polls at No. 18. Then came a match-up with top-ranked Notre Dame at old Notre Dame Stadium.

"You walk into this old, crappy stadium that has so much history," recalls Giannetti, "and if you didn't know what Notre Dame football was all about, you would say, 'Oh, my God, this is the ugliest stadium I've ever seen.' And then to make it even worse, they put the visitors in a locker room that's about the size of a family room. You've got 60 guys all cramped in this locker room that probably should only hold about half of that.

"And it's funny, you always see the sign on the way out to the field that says, 'Play like a champion today,' and the Notre Dame players all hit it. I don't know who did it, but one of the guys on our team wrote right by the doorway as we were coming out, 'Play better than a champion today.' And it was pretty cool. As we were walking out, we were hitting that."

The game received plenty of attention from the national media.

"They were 10-0, pretty much signed to play Colorado in the Orange Bowl for the national championship," says Giannett. "We were ranked No. 18."

No problem. The Nittany Lions beat the Irish, 24-21, in a victory that is considered one of the greatest in Penn State history.

"In the first half, they basically did what they wanted on offense," Giannetti recalls. "And in the second half, we just came out and shut them down. I mean, if they got 10 yards in that second half, they got a lot. And then our offense got going."

The Lions then beat Pitt before a close loss to Florida State in the Blockbuster Bowl in Giannetti's final game at Penn State. Then it was on to the pros. Giannetti was selected by the Indianapolis Colts in the 1991 NFL draft. He played with Indianapolis on and off for about two years. After his second year in Indianapolis, he signed as a free agent with the Atlanta Falcons. While with the Falcons, he suffered a torn bicep and was placed on injured reserve.

"It knocked me out of doing anything athletic or physical for about six to eight months," Giannetti says. "So I tried to come back after that, and it didn't go as well as I thought."

Giannetti next played for a Canadian Football League team that was based in San Antonio, Texas, and later with an Arena Football League team in Albany.

"At that point, I was getting into coaching a little bit in the school district that I teach in now," Giannetti says. "There were some opportunities to do some things, so I pretty much decided to get a real job."

Now, Giannetti relives his Penn State experience every day in one way or another with the high school players he coaches. He has also gone back to Penn State to give coaching clinics.

"As coaches we tell the kids that not only are you playing the best game in the world, but that this game will teach you everything about life," says Giannetti, who has a young son with his wife, Dora. "Football will teach you to work as a team. It will teach you how to fight through adversity and tough times."

Giannetti knows that as much as anyone.

BRIAN GELZHEISER

The 1994 Penn State team had one of the greatest offensive seasons in college football history. However, Brian Gelzheiser is here to make a case for the defense, which hardly anyone mentions.

Gelzheiser led the team with 126 tackles to finish his career with 315, second on the all-time Penn State list behind only Greg Buttle. Part of the reason for Gelzheiser's success had to be all those rough practice sessions he went through against the high-powered first-team offense.

"How would you like to go up against those guys every day in practice?" Gelzheiser asks rhetorically. "It got old."

The 1994 Lions outscored opponents 526 to 232. They broke nearly every school offense record and set a couple NCAA marks for total offense (520.2 yards a game) and points per game (47.8).

"You look at the offense and you had one of the biggest tight ends in college football at the time, Kyle Brady. It wasn't fun. You try to tackle someone 6-7, 270 pounds," says Gelzheiser.

But Gelzheiser went after offensive players with unabashed glee. And it didn't matter how big they were. His head-rattling hits could be heard all over the field, and usually in the stadium seats as well.

"I think sometimes I can have an interception," Gelzheiser once told a reporter for the school newspaper, the *Penn State Collegian*, "but I'd rather hit them."

Gelzheiser, who now works in sales in the Pittsburgh area for an orthopedic company, recalls that great Penn State team with fondness. And who wouldn't? All the 1994 Lions did was go 12-0 and win the first Rose Bowl game in school history. The season did have its drawbacks for Gelzheiser, though.

"The average scoring time was less than two minutes, so needless to say, the defense was on the field all game long," he says. "So the offense would play two minutes, and then get a five-minute break. They played two minutes, we played five.

"Honestly, if you looked at the amount of plays that they ran, compared to the amount of plays that the defense was on the field, it wasn't even close. The only good part about it was that they scored so much that I only really played two full games, because by halftime, I was pretty much done, anyway."

Gelzheiser was a top two-sport athlete at Baldwin High School in Pittsburgh—a quarterback and safety in football and a pitcher in baseball.

BRIAN GELZHEISER

Years lettered: 1991, 1992, 1993 and 1994
Position: Linebacker
Accomplishments: Top tackler in both 1993 an 1994.
Finished career as the second-leading tackler in
Penn State history with 315 tackles.

"I went to Penn State because of Jerry Sandusky [Joe Paterno's assistant]," Gelzheiser says. "I had gone to their football camp and I liked it."

He also enjoyed his relationship with strength coach John Thomas because "he made you work hard." Gelzheiser calls Thomas "one of the most influential coaches at Penn State when I played."

Since he had never played linebacker, Gelzheiser was red-shirted in his freshman year in 1990 so he could learn the position. There were signs of greatness before he became a full-time starter in 1993. Against Notre Dame in 1992, Gelzheiser was called upon when starter Brett Wright was injured. He made a game-high 15 tackles, but one play stood out among the rest when Gelzheiser was on special teams. Covering a kickoff, he flattened the kick returner with a vicious shot, separating him from the ball. He also separated the runner from his shoulder.

"We lost that game [17-16] by a two-point conversion that they scored," Gelzheiser recalls. "But I think, for myself, that was one of my best games."

That smash-mouth style continued in Gelzheiser's red-shirt junior year in 1993. And he didn't miss a start, leading the team with 113 tackles despite playing the whole season with bone chips in his ankle. That season, incidentally, was the year that Penn State made the transition from an independent to the Big Ten.

"I think the big difference was that it was a more physical type of game," Gelzheiser says. "You felt beat up when you were done. And the offensive linemen were a lot bigger."

Gelzheiser also saw a difference in Penn State's recruiting philosophy.

"Joe never wanted the offensive linemen to weigh more than 275, 280 pounds, and then towards the end of my career you saw the first 300-pound guy like Keith Conlin and Wayne Holmes. They were 300 when they came in as freshmen."

The Lions completed their first season in the Big Ten with a 6-2 record in the league. Overall, they were 10-2, including a victory over Tennessee in the Citrus Bowl.

Gelzheiser found that the traveling was easier than playing as an independent.

"We would fly all over the country as an independent," he says. "In the Big Ten, the farthest we would go was Minnesota."

Then came the remarkable 1994 season. The Lions opened with a 56-3 rout of Minnesota. That type of score became more and more common as the Lions rolled over their opponents week after week. In their first five games, they racked up 254 points. Although Penn State's scoring was up, Paterno kept the Nittany Lions' feet on the ground.

"Joe did a good job of keeping us humble," Gelzheiser remembers. "He always told us we weren't any good. It was always, 'You guys aren't as good as you think you are.' We were constantly not only trying to prove to ourselves that we were any good, but trying to keep him happy and prove to him that we were a good team."

The Lions didn't have many close calls. One of them was a comeback 35-31 victory over Illinois in Champaign as Penn State rallied from a 21-0 deficit in the first quarter. By the end of the season, Penn State headed to the Rose Bowl against Oregon with an 11-0 record. The Lions were ranked No. 2 in the national polls behind Nebraska.

Their dreams of a national championship died, though, even before they took the field. The night before the Rose Bowl game, Nebraska won its bowl game to clinch the title. Gelzheiser says he and his teammates were very upset.

"I can remember going down to a meeting. We had a meeting right before bed check, and Joe called everyone down and basically said, 'Obviously it's not the way we wanted it to work, they gave it away. But what we're going to do is just go out and play and show them who is the best team in the country.'"

The Lions made a statement, beating a very good Oregon team that had won the Pac-12 title, 38-20.

"I could tell you in that game, we were mad," Gelzheiser says. "We were playing angry. With the leadership we had on that team, we were able to funnel that aggravation that we had and just play. There was no doubt in my mind that we would win that game."

It was a landmark victory for Paterno, who passed Bear Bryant for number one in bowl victories. Gelzheiser was among a group of players who crashed Paterno's press conference to hand him the game ball.

"They didn't want to let us in," Gelzheiser recalls, "but Joe said something and they let us in."

After school, Gelzheiser played some pro football with the Indianapolis Colts and the Amsterdam Admirals of NFL Europe. He also did some pitching for the Kansas City Royals. Finally, a football injury cut short his pro career.

Now out of the game, he still manages to be part of the Penn State scene. He goes back for games when he can. And he has played in Sandusky's Second Mile Celebrity Golf Classic, a charity that benefits children.

"Brian's a real nice guy and was a heck of a football player," says Kerry Collins, quarterback of the great 1994 Penn State team. "He was a great leader for the time. He was really the cornerstone of that (1994) defense."

MARK TATE

Why would anyone want to be a cornerback? That player runs the risk of being bumped by a 300-pound lineman, burned on pass coverage or buried under a pile of players. It's one of the least glamorous and scariest positions in football.

Mark Tate, though, might raise his hand when asked that question. Tate likes a good challenge. No, he lives for it. And at Penn State in the nineties, he quietly developed into one of the top cornerbacks of his era—good enough to later play professional football on two continents and in several countries.

No matter that Tate had been a star running back from one of the top high school football programs in America, Erie (Pennsylvania) Cathedral Prep. Tate didn't care which position he played in college, he just wanted to contribute.

Now working in sales for a pharmaceutical company, Tate recalls when he was trying to crack the talented Penn State lineup at a crucial time in Nittany Lion history. It was in 1993, Tate's red-shirt freshman year, that the Lions were making the transition from an independent to the Big Ten.

"It was fun to be there at the beginning," Tate says. "I can remember the first year of going to the Big Ten, there was a lot of speculation as to how we would do. A lot of people didn't think we could deal with the toughness and the size of the Big Ten, but we did well that year. But the Big Ten was definitely a tough conference. There was really not a week you could take off."

Tate played in all the Lions' games in '93 and made his first career interception, against Illinois. Then, in 1994 he made the starting lineup and almost immediately began to turn heads. Against Rutgers in an early-season game, he made five tackles, sacked the Scarlet Knights' quarterback for a four-yard loss and forced a fumble that led to a touchdown. That year, Penn State ran the table in the Big Ten and ended up with an undefeated season and a Rose Bowl triumph over Oregon. The Lions finished with a 12-0 record and No. 2 ranking in the country.

"That entire season was magical," Tate recalls. "It's what you come to Penn State for, to go undefeated, have a shot at the national title and play in the Rose Bowl. You always hear about the Rose Bowl. And once we got there, it definitely lived up to our expectations.

"We were only disappointed that we weren't playing for the national title, because as players you like to win a football game on the field, not have somebody vote for you."

Nebraska was voted the nation's No. 1 team the night before Penn State played in the Rose Bowl.

MARK TATE

Years lettered: 1993, 1994, 1995 and 1996
Position: Cornerback
Accomplishments: Established himself as one of top cornerbacks in the Big Ten in 1995 when he made 52 tackles.

In 1995, Tate established himself as one of the top right cornerbacks in the Big Ten, making 52 tackles. It was the result of a strong work ethic and his undying dedication to excellence. What he lacked in size (six feet, 177 pounds), Tate made up for in toughness.

"I just wanted to consistently improve my skills each year, so I stayed at school during the summers, trained and exercised and went all the way through," he says. "You get the best workout in the summer. And after practice, I worked hard on my open-field tackling."

Writers talk about Tate's performances against Michigan and Auburn (in the Outback Bowl) that season. But Tate thinks he had a better game against Ohio State, even though it was a loss.

"It was at our place and Ohio State was loaded that year," Tate remembers. "They had Eddie George. He won the Heisman Trophy. And they had wide receiver Terry Glenn. He was one of the best wide receivers in football that year. I had a good game against him . . . a couple big plays on fourth down. I think that was one of my best games as a collegian, because I was playing against the best receiver and I had a good game."

Tate continued to impress pro scouts in 1996 with his toughness and smart play as Penn State rolled up an 11-2 record, including a decisive victory over Texas in the Fiesta Bowl. The 16 seniors in Tate's class finished with a 42-7 record and four bowl victories.

"We were the winningest class in school history," Tate points out.

Right after graduation, Tate signed a free agent contract with the New England Patriots.

"I was on their practice squad for a year," he says. "The NFL experience was a contrast to the way Joe ran his program. In the college atmosphere, you kind of get to know your teammates and make friends. In the pros, it's like a guy's here today and gone tomorrow. You're competing against each other."

Tate next tried the Canadian Football League for a year, playing for the Saskatchewan Rough Riders.

"I figured this was my dream," he says. "When I was young I wanted to pursue it. I didn't necessarily know I was going to go to Canada. But I went there and had a good time."

Tate later came back to the States and hooked up with the Philadelphia Eagles, then later joined the XFL where an old Penn State teammate, Wally Richardson, was also playing.

"Again, it was football, it was a brand new league and, you know, it was another opportunity to continue playing."

When the XFL folded, Tate went to Europe to play for the Amsterdam Admirals. Next stop after NFL Europe: training camp with the Oakland Raiders. When Tate was cut by the Raiders, he decided to quit football and get a job with a pharmaceutical company. Tate, who has three children with his wife, Erin, also began work on an MBA.

He managed to fit in his interview for this book in the midst of three days of intensive meetings at work that lasted late into the night. In his business career, Tate continues to apply lessons learned from Penn State. For instance, he makes sure that he's never late for any meeting or appointment. That goes back to the squad meetings with Paterno when the team would go over the game plan.

Mark Tate lives in Pennsylvania with his wife, Erin,
and three children and works in pharmaceutical sales.
Photo courtesy of Mark Tate

"At Penn State the meeting starts at nine, and everybody's in his seat at 8:45," Tate recalls. "It's like you're afraid to ever be late. It's a good habit, and I'm definitely grateful. I'm always at least 15 to 20 minutes early, and everybody knows it's just a habit from my football days at Penn State."

KERRY COLLINS

K erry Collins, the quarterback, was talking about Kerry Collins, the rancher.

"After the season, I go to my ranch and work," Collins says. "It's a working cattle operation. So the work starts when I get back there."

"There" is a 1,600-acre ranch in North Carolina. Collins, a Penn State star in the '90s and now a quarterback for the Oakland Raiders, seems to have as much fun ranching as playing football.

"There hasn't been anything I've enjoyed more than getting my farm started, being down there, working, being a part of that," he says. "It's what I want to do after I'm finished playing."

Considering the recent upswing in his pro football career, that might be a while.

Released by the New York Giants after the 2003 season, the gifted quarterback hooked on with the Raiders as a free agent. He took over as a starter after Rich Gannon was injured, and put on some dazzling performances in 2004. One of his best: A comeback 25-24 win in snowy Denver in which Collins completed 26 of 45 passes for 339 yards, including four touchdowns. That was in the middle of a strong three-game stretch against AFC West opponents. All Collins did was average 303 yards a game, throw nine TD passes and complete 61.2 per cent of his attempts.

"It took about four or five games to get to know the offense really well, go out and execute it," Collins says. "I felt more comfortable with what we were doing, and I got more confidence in going into the games and with my preparation during the week.

"I worked hard. That's the bottom line. I worked at it, and starting clicking a lot better, started getting more familiarity with my receivers and coaches. It started paying off toward the end of the year."

His success had to remind Oakland coaches of Collins's playoff performances in the 2000 season with the Giants, particularly the game that he calls the greatest of his pro career. Or, a Penn State fan might remember Collins's performance in 1994, when he led the greatest offensive juggernaut in Nittany Lion history. The 1994 season was the culmination of a dream fulfilled for Collins, who grew up wanting to play for Penn State. Collins had played football at Wilson High School in West Lawn, Pennsylvania, just outside of Reading.

"I wasn't heavily recruited by a lot of the major schools," Collins recalls. "But certainly, when Penn State started recruiting me, obviously being from Pennsylvania, I knew what they were all about.

KERRY COLLINS

Years lettered: 1992, 1993 and 1994
Position: Quarterback
Accomplishments: In 1994, won the Maxwell Award (nation's outstanding player) and the Davey O'Brien Award (nation's top quarterback). A consensus All-American, he broke a slew of Penn State records in 1994, including passing yards (2,679), completions (176) and completion percentage (66.7). Finished No. 4 on the all-time Penn State passing list with 5,304 yards.

"And when it came down to making a decision, I really couldn't do any better than that. It was the best place I could go."

It wasn't until early in the 1993 season, Collins's junior year, that he won the starting job at quarterback.

"I replaced John Sacca in maybe the third or fourth game," Collins recalls.

It was the final game of the regular season that Penn State fans will remember for a long time, though. Penn State trailed Michigan State 37-17 late in the third quarter at East Lansing. It seemed hopeless for Penn State. But the Lions scored three straight touchdowns, two on passes by Collins, to pull out a wild 38-37 victory.

"Michigan State was a tough place to play," Collins says. "But we had gotten better throughout the year, and we really seemed to click in that game.

"I remember hitting Bobby Engram on a couple of long passes. Kyle Brady played a big part in that game. There were guys who were instrumental in winning that game that ultimately were going to be big players going into '94. I think that game was really the one that spring-boarded us into believing that we could be a championship team."

The Lions gained even more confidence with an impressive 31-13 victory over Tennessee in the Citrus Bowl.

"Guys were emerging," Collins says. "I was coming into my own, and Bobby Engram, Kyle Brady, Ki-Jana Carter were young guys who had played and all of a sudden were becoming good players.

"We really started to come on at the end of the year. So I think the seeds were sewn for a lot of excitement for '94."

The Nittany Lions opened the 1994 season with a 56-3 victory at Minnesota. They followed that with a 38-14 triumph over Southern Cal, and a 61-21 trouncing of Iowa. Later in the season they handed Ohio State one of its worst losses in history, 63-14.

"The game that really stands out was the Ohio State game at home. They were a top twenty team. It was obviously a big game, and we really put it to them. We just dominated them from the start. I think that game was probably our best game of the year."

All this happened in just Penn State's second year in the Big Ten.

"We were new to the conference, and so I think the best thing we did was just try to get as prepared as we could for every game," Collins says. "We would go out and play our best game every Saturday.

"When we got through the first couple of games, and put up the kind of points we did, I think we tried to live up to that standard every time we went out. It was just one of those things where we kept getting better and better."

Not everything was easy for the Lions, however. Against Illinois at Champaign, they fell behind 21-0 early and rallied for a 35-31 victory to clinch their first Big Ten title and a Rose Bowl berth. It was the biggest winning comeback in Joe Paterno's 29 years as head coach at Penn State.

"Our confident attitude carried us through some of the tough spots in the season," Collins says, "and we were able to get the big wins on the road."

In the Rose Bowl, the Lions completed their perfect season with a 38-20 victory over Oregon. They finished No. 2 in the country behind Nebraska, but you could certainly make a case they were No. 1. Paterno did, declaring his team "national champions."

Kerry Collins is a quarterback for the Oakland Raiders. He and his wife
Brooke have a daughter, Riley, and live in North Carolina in the off-season.
Photo courtesy of the Oakland Raiders

Offensively, no college team in the nation did what Penn State did that season—or any season. The Nittany Lions set NCAA records for scoring with 47.8 points a game and for total offense with an average of 520.2 yards a game. Collins set a Penn State record for a season by passing for 2,679 yards. His yardage average of 10.15 a throw is still a Penn State record.

"There was a lot of talent surrounding me, but probably the best group that didn't get a lot of attention was the offensive line," Collins says. "We had an unbelievable offensive line."

Collins singles out Bucky Greeley, Jeff Hartings, Marco Rivera, Keith Conlin and Andre Johnson.

"They weren't just good at one thing. They were excellent at both passing and run blocking, so that was probably what made the whole thing go for our offense. It allowed me to have time to make throws and allowed Ki-Jana Carter to have big holes to run through.

"They were very intelligent guys, worked extremely hard, and took a lot of pride in what they did. It was probably the best offensive line in college football that year."

While the Penn State defense didn't get the same kind of attention as the offense, it played an important role in the season's accomplishments. Linebacker Brian Gelzheiser was one of the key defensive players, leading the Lions in tackles in 1994 for the second straight year.

"Our defense came up with a lot of big plays," Collins remembers. "So much attention was on the offense that year that you didn't hear about the defense. I was just thinking about the Michigan game [a 31-24 victory at Ann Arbor]. They made some big plays at the end of the game, some big stops. You can't go 12-0 and win the Rose Bowl without having a good defense."

The next football game that Collins played was in a professional uniform. He was the first draft pick of the expansion Carolina Panthers.

In his first start early in the 1995 NFL season, Collins hardly looked like a rookie. He completed 18 of 32 passes for 233 yards. He threw his first NFL touchdown pass on a four-yarder to Pete Metzelaars.

Collins played three years with Carolina and another year with New Orleans before joining the New York Giants in 1999. One year later, Collins had the Giants in the Super Bowl.

Along the way he played what he considered the greatest game of his pro career. Facing the Minnesota Vikings in the NFC championship game at Giants Stadium on January 14, 2001, Collins completed 28 of 39 passes for 381 yards and five touchdowns. The five TDs tied Sid Luckman's NFL mark set in 1943. His 381 passing yards broke Troy Aikman's NFC championship record of 380 set in 1994. And his 28 completions broke the Giants' team record.

And Collins didn't even play the fourth quarter!

"It was just one of those days where everything went my way," Collins says. "It was a great atmosphere, a championship game at home, and it was just a lot of fun."

Not even a loss to Baltimore in the Super Bowl could diminish Collins's Hall of Fame performance. In his renewed football life in Oakland in 2004, Collins was starting to find things going his way again.

"I really started to respond to what Norv Turner was doing in his play calling," Collins says of the Oakland coach. "You know, it took a little while. It took four, five games, but once I got it going, I felt like I played pretty well."

After the season, Collins went back to his North Carolina ranch to refresh himself.

"I really believe in rest," Collins says. "And so for most of January and February and on into March, I try to get away from football as much as I can. It's such a long season, and your body takes a beating, and I really feel like the best thing for me is to be away from the game for a while."

It is there on the ranch where Collins spends quality time with his wife, Brooke, and their baby girl, Riley.

"It's great," Collins says. "It's been unbelievable. I just look at [my daughter], and wonder what I ever did without her. It completely changes your view on the world, but in an overwhelmingly positive way.

"I mean, that's the great thing about it, you come home after a tough game, and she doesn't care, she doesn't know anything about football. She's just happy that she has her dad. That's a special feeling."

Now it's Kerry Collins, the quarterback, talking about Kerry Collins, the dad.

WALLY RICHARDSON

Have football, will travel.

"I definitely had some frequent flyer miles," Wally Richardson says, reflecting on a professional football career that took him to two continents, four leagues and a number of countries.

Going long distances was nothing new for Richardson, a strong-armed quarterback at Penn State in the mid-'90s who was known for his often spectacular touchdown drives. Many still remember the legendary last-gasp drive he made against Michigan State as a junior at Penn State in 1995. And now Richardson, the sixth leading passer in school history, has made the full circle back to Penn State. He works for the university as an academic counselor for football players.

Looking back on a football career that, at times, seemed like a roller coaster ride, Richardson knew at a very young age that he wanted to be a quarterback. As far back as he could remember growing up in Sumter, South Carolina, that was basically the only position he played.

"I punted a little when I was in middle school and also did some short snaps, just to do it," Richardson says. "But I never played a down of defense in my life."

What led him to University Park from the Deep South?

"I wanted to go to school away from home," he says by phone from his office in the Lasch Football Building on the Penn State campus. "I also wanted to have a chance to play for a national championship."

By the time Richardson and his fellow seniors had graduated, they had posted a 42-7 record and four bowl victories. As a starter, Richardson had a 21-5 record. He arrived at Penn State in 1992, but generally didn't see any meaningful action until he was the Lions' starting quarterback in 1995. And that season was quite a ride. Losses to Wisconsin and Ohio State and then later to Northwestern had derailed any Penn State plans to get back to the Rose Bowl. But the Lions had beaten Michigan, a Top 20 team.

They faced another stern test the week after at Michigan State and things didn't look good for the Lions late in the game. They were losing 20-17 with the ball on their own 27-yard line. There was only 1:45 left. Penn State had no timeouts left. As Richardson stepped into the huddle, he faced long yardage, long odds and perhaps a long ride home. All he had to do was act like John Elway, the king of the comeback quarterbacks.

"We were backed up pretty good," Richardson says. "If we didn't score on that last drive, we probably still would have gone to a bowl game, but it wouldn't have been a New Year's Day bowl. So that's what our motivation was at that point."

WALLY RICHARDSON

Years lettered: 1992, 1994, 1995 and 1996
Position: Quarterback
Accomplishments: Sixth leading passer in Penn State history with 4,419 yards. Set school records for season completions (193 in 1995), season pass attempts (335 in 1995) and game completions (33 vs. Wisconsin in 1995).

The ball was in Richardson's hands. First down—73 yards to go.

"My thinking was, just get first downs," he says. "As long as you're picking up first downs, the clock is going to stop. So when you're hustling up to the ball, while they're spotting the ball, you can tell people what you want to run.

"You have to play at a little faster pace . . . just don't forget what you've been doing, and don't forget your assignment. As long as people take care of their assignments, things usually have a way of working out."

Richardson started moving Penn State down the field.

"We had a play where Mike Archie would run out into the flat. They were playing zone coverage and just giving up the flat, so I kept throwing that pass.

"But the big play on that drive was the last play of the game. The last two plays of the drive were the same plays. It was a 'Double Read Screen.' I could throw to Mike Archie, a sideline pass, and he could outflank the defenders to the corner of the end zone. We also had a little middle screen to the receiver coming down the line of scrimmage where he could get in there, catch the ball in the middle of the field and go towards the end zone."

Richardson first threw to Archie.

"We ended up getting some good yardage, but we came up a little short, just inside the five."

Paterno then told Richardson to throw the ball to Bobby Engram. He did.

"When Bobby caught the ball, there were two or three guys around him and he had to fight into the end zone. He actually ducked up under a tackle to slide into the end zone, and that's how that one ended up."

Final: Penn State 24, Michigan State 20.

Richardson's masterful handling of those final two minutes ended up in Penn State lore. It is simply known as "The Drive" to many Nittany Lion fans of that era.

Penn State wound up achieving their goal: a New Year's Day bowl. Richardson sparked a 43-14 victory over Auburn in the Outback Bowl to finish off a 9-3 season. And this one was personal, a revenge motive going back to high school, as Richardson remembers.

"The tailback for Auburn at that time was Stephen Davis, who plays for the Carolina Panthers now," Richardson says. "He was from South Carolina also. He was a great sprint champion in high school. We were 14-0 playing his team for the state championship and we lost. So we ended our season 14-1. That was one of the more bitter pills I had [to swallow] on the playing field up to that point in my life. So I definitely wanted to beat them because that was a little payback for me.

"The game was played in a torrential downpour. The drainage at the Big Sombrero stadium in Tampa wasn't really good, and we played in a lot of mud. But we ended up roughing them up pretty good."

Richardson completed 13 of 24 passes for 217 yards and four touchdowns, with only one interception.

Richardson had great expectations for the team and himself as the Lions prepared for the 1996 season. The team got off to a good start, but Richardson didn't.

*Wally Richardson lives in the State College area and works
as a counselor for football players at Penn State.*
Photo courtesy of Wally Richardson

"I didn't have the type of numbers that I thought I should have had and was kind of maligned throughout the year," Richardson recalls. "I even got benched at Indiana. We were playing Northwestern at home the next weekend.

"There was some discussion as to whether I should start or Mike McQueary should start. Joe Paterno pulled me into his office when we got back that week and told me, 'Wally, I just made a change [in the game against Indiana] and I thought that's what I needed to do at the time. But you're my quarterback, you're going to start against Northwestern this week.'

"I had really been upset after that whole thing at Indiana and when he told me that, I was fired up for the next weekend."

It wasn't going to be an easy game for Penn State. The Wildcats had a lot of players back from their Rose Bowl team of the year before.

"I just remember playing them in the snow and we had a packed house," Richardson says. "One of the first passes I threw almost got picked off. But then on that same drive, I threw a bomb that Joe Jurevicius caught and we kind of took it from there."

Final: Penn State 34, Northwestern 9.

"It was a really gratifying win for the team and me, too," Richardson says.

Richardson later finished off an 11-2 season by leading a 38-15 triumph over Texas in the Fiesta Bowl. Following his last season at Penn State in 1996, Richardson was drafted by the Baltimore Ravens of the NFL. The Ravens sent Richardson to Europe to play for the England Monarchs to gain more playing experience.

"I didn't see as much action as I thought I was going to see. I started the season off as the starter and I got pulled at halftime, and I can't remember if I played a game in five or six weeks," Richardson says. "The next significant action I saw was in the last game of the season."

That was against the Barcelona Dragons. Josh LaRocca, the Monarchs' starting quarterback, was injured early in the game. Richardson replaced him and completed his first pass for a 31-yard touchdown play. Then in the third quarter, Richardson fired another TD pass, this one covering 23 yards.

Not a bad day overall: 12 for 14 with two TD passes.

"I was glad to just get in and show people what I'm capable of," Richardson says.

Richardson found the European experience enlightening in his one year of play.

"It was a little different," Richardson says. "The games were always well attended, and they were into the games. The most knowledgeable fans were the German fans. They really had a pretty good understanding of the game."

The Monarch football team lived at the Crystal Palace, a dormitory-style building where Olympian athletes trained. It wasn't exactly the Ritz and the food wasn't always to Richardson's liking, either.

"I didn't take to English food too well. I pretty much would eat a lot of potatoes and bread over there. I didn't get down with the liver pudding and all that."

Richardson came back to the States and rejoined the Ravens. He was in Baltimore for the 1997 and 1998 seasons before joining the Atlanta Falcons in 1999.

Richardson would later play in the XFL and the Arena Football League. He enjoyed his experience in both leagues, especially the innovative XFL.

"That was the first league to have reporters in the locker room before the game," Richardson says. "Fans got to see what coaches were saying to their teams. They had the aerial camera, where you get to see the action from up top. The NFL is doing that stuff now. The XFL kind of brought that to the forefront."

Richardson battled through a knee injury to later play for the Los Angeles Avengers of the Arena Football League.

"My intentions were to go back out there the next season, but they made a decision to release me. By that point, I made a decision to get my master's degree and get into the next phase of my life."

Which was working for Penn State.

"I've been working here as a full-time counselor." Richardson says. "I basically help guys get their schedules together and I also make sure they're eligible to play football."

Many years after leaving Penn State, Richardson is still finding a way to make an impact on the football program.

CHUCK FRANZETTA

A sk Chuck Franzetta about Penn State football and the stories never stop coming. Scratch him and you're almost sure he would bleed blue and white. So where else would you find the former Penn State player on a fall day than tailgating outside Beaver Stadium? Franzetta and his wife, Jean, were entertaining visitors at an elaborate food fest. Franzetta, who wore Nittany Lion Blue in the '60s, was luxuriating in the friendships of other former players in the Lettermen's Lot.

"Jean likes to get a good spot on game days," Franzetta says. "So if you're staying at our house, be prepared to get up early."

Franzetta embodies the true spirit of Penn State football, as his story shows. Today he is president and CEO of Franzetta & Associates, a consulting firm dealing with logistics for a variety of businesses. His background is impressive: He was once a star for the Flying Tigers, an international cargo airline. He helped the company rise to the position of number-one cargo carrying airline in the world. Yet, in the '60s he was just trying to find a place on the Penn State football team.

"I grew up in a little steel mill town called Midland in western Pennsylvania, right on the Ohio and West Virginia borders," Franzetta says. "Sports were a way out, just as it was for all those kids coming out of the coal mines and steel mill towns, and some of the farms. Sports were your way for a different form of life."

Franzetta's way out took him to Penn State, where he ended up a defensive end.

"They wanted me to play center," Franzetta recalls, "but I was too small and too skinny."

Franzetta also had another problem: mononucleosis. He battled through the disease before getting his chance with the varsity. He had lost a lot of weight, and went home between his freshman and sophomore years to bulk up.

CHUCK FRANZETTA

Years lettered: 1968
Position: Defensive end

*Chuck Franzetta runs a consulting firm in the State College area deal-
ing with logistics for a variety of businesses. He and wife Jean can usually be found in the Lettermen's Lot at Penn State football games.*
Photo courtesy of Chuck Franzetta

The bout with mono, an injury to his toe in a factory accident and a series of other injuries had clouded Franzetta's future as a football player. No sooner would he work his way up to second team defensive end than he would drop down again. He didn't give up. Franzetta dealt with adversity the only way he knew how as a defensive end: He blocked it out.

Franzetta was on the practice field one day getting ready for a game when he was injured.

"I got caught in a situation where one of my shoulders got ripped out," Franzetta recalls. "They used to come out every day, I wouldn't tell anybody. Either the right or the left would come out and I would just shove it back in myself. But in this particular situation, it was one of those really bad ones, where I couldn't do anything. The doctor had to come get me."

In a couple of weeks, Franzetta had sufficiently recovered, allowing him to get back on the practice field.

"I was at last team again," he says.

That hadn't stopped Franzetta before.

"Right before the Boston College game, I got moved up to second team again," Franzetta says. "I was there on the sideline and just feeling really good."

Suddenly, one of the starters was forced to come out of the game with an injury.

"There was this grad assistant who turned around and said, 'Defensive end.' Well, the guy who was supposed to go before me didn't move. I got up off my knees and stepped back behind him and ran around him. So I went in, got in on a couple of tackles and then came back out.

"Somebody came up and said, 'You weren't supposed to be in.' I said, 'Yeah, well, I know.' So we're back in the same situation later in the game. The other guy got hurt from the other side and the kid did the same thing, 'Defensive end.' I did the same thing. I got up, stepped back, ran around, went in. That was a kick."

The following week, Franzetta dislocated each of his shoulders a couple of times during practice.

"At this one point, my left shoulder was out of the socket and I couldn't get it back in," Franzetta remembers. "So I was trying to play off my right side, and between plays I was trying to get it to go back in, and I happened to glance up and I saw the team doctor on the sidelines. And I could tell he was looking at me, and all of a sudden I saw him coming. I was like, 'Ah, damn.'

"He came right up to me and he looked at me, and he didn't even try to help me at that point. He said, 'Your left shoulder's out of the socket, isn't it?' I said, 'Yeah'. By now I was really in bad pain. And he grabbed my jersey, on my right arm, and he said, 'Come with me,'

The doctor dragged Franzetta right over to Joe Paterno.

"As a physician in good conscience, I can't allow this to go on any longer," the doctor told the Penn State coach. "He refuses to quit. I'm quitting for him."

Paterno looked at Franzetta and said:

"Charley, he's the boss."

Franzetta now reflects: "And that was it. That was my shot. I had gotten hurt repeatedly. I literally was taped from head to toe, both knees, elbow, both shoulders, rib, nose, the whole bit, and they told me I couldn't play."

He wasn't finished with football, though. In his junior and senior seasons, he worked as a drill center for the Lions so that the centers could get their hitting in. He also helped to coach the freshmen.

After school, Franzetta joined the business world as general manager of the Flying Tigers. He later moved over to *Newsweek* as director of worldwide distribution for the magazine giant. Franzetta also found time to teach logistics at Penn State, lecture at numerous colleges and start up his own business.

When he was named the youngest general manager at the Flying Tigers organization, Franzetta wrote letters to two people who were meaningful in his life—his assistant high school coach and Paterno.

"I told Joe that it was a number of the things at Penn State that helped me: the focus on planning, on doing things right, of dealing with detail to which other people weren't paying attention," Franzetta says. "It was the commitment to just keep going at it, going at it, the general characteristics that you learned in that environment . . . the pride. You turn around, and you did it the right way."

There wasn't much more to say, except:

We are . . . Penn State!